Food Processor Cookbook
A Revolution in Modern Cooking

Tony Schmaeling

Food Processor Cookbook
A Revolution in Modern Cooking

Tony Schmaeling

Photography Howard Jones
Food for Photography Joan Campbell
Design John and Penelope Lee

 CHARTWELL BOOKS INC.

Published by Chartwell Books Inc.
A Division of Book Sales Inc.
110 Enterprise Avenue
Secaucus, New Jersey 07094

Acknowledgements

Our grateful thanks to June Hazell of The Bay Tree and to Giftmakers for supplying the many attractive items of tableware from their shops for use in the photographs.

This edition
Published by Chartwell Books Inc.
A Division of Book Sales Inc.
110 Enterprise Avenue
Secaucus, New Jersey 07094

First published by Paul Hamlyn Pty Limited
176 South Creek Road, Dee Why West, Australia 2099
First published 1979
© Copyright Paul Hamlyn Pty Limited
Produced in Australia by the Publisher
Typeset in Australia by G.T. Setters Pty Limited
Printed by Tien Mah Press (Pte) Limited
2 Jalan Jentera, Jurong Town Singapore 22
ISBN: 0-89009-303-2

Contents

Introduction

The appearance in 1972 on the kitchen appliance market of the first food processor opened up for the amateur cook new vistas into a field of cuisine until then the sole preserve of the professional chef.

Recipes which in the past belonged to the realm of culinary literature, interesting to read but never to be attempted, suddenly became possible.

Gone was the dreary, tearful task of chopping onions, the arm tiring job of puréeing through a sieve, the messy business of pastry making and the frustrations of a curdled mayonnaise.

Dinner parties and festive occasions, modest family snacks and even that meal-by-oneself were now more easily prepared and because of the time saved, could be more elaborate and interesting.

Speed of operation and the ease with which the food processor could be handled, made it an immediate success. Today there are many versions of the original implement and all of them, in similar ways, serve the amateur as well as the professional. Its versatility is such that about the only job the processor is unable to do is to whip egg whites.

The recipes in this book have been selected to show how easy it is to use the processor and how the previously difficult and time consuming jobs are speedily done. The examples shown here will serve as an inspiration to attempt many other recipes never tried before. Newly found methods will provide easy ways of overcoming some of the problems experienced in the past.

 Processor

How to use the food processor

It is most important from the very beginning to understand the nature of the food processor. The speed with which it does the various jobs is what distinguishes it from all other appliances. This fact may take some time to accept but once realised, the rest is simple. Seconds now, not minutes and the job is done.

One of the most frequently used terms in the text is the instruction 'process' and depending on the type of blade or disc used, it may mean chop, mince, mix, grate, etc. Once the food processor has become second nature to you, the selection of the correct attachment will become obvious.

Next to the name of every recipe are the symbols showing the type of appliance and attachment used in the text. In the description of the method the symbol ● indicates the use of the processor in this particular step.

All food processors have at least the following attachments and this is what they will do for you:

 Stainless Steel Blade

1. The stainless steel blade, undoubtedly the most frequently used and the most useful of the attachments. When chopping and mixing ingredients of different consistencies start with the hardest consistency, e.g. meat first, then add vegetables, which will be chopped and mixed. The blade will:

chop vegetables, herbs and parsleys, fruit.
Cut the ingredients into approximately 2½ cm (1 in) rough cubes and process, 2 cups at a time, to the required texture. Most ingredients will be chopped in less than 5 seconds. Stop the processor frequently to check the fineness obtained.

mince raw or cooked meat.

Cut the meat into approximately 2½ cm (1 in) rough cubes and process, 1½ cups at a time, to the required fineness. Raw meat will need 5-10 seconds mincing and cooked meat 3-5 seconds.

make Pastry, dough or cake mixes.

Place all the dry ingredients, 1½ cups at a time, together with the chilled shortening into the work bowl and process until it is the texture of breadcrumbs. While processing, add the liquid through the feed tube. In a few seconds the pastry will form into a ball. Do not over-process.

purée vegetables, fruit, fish and meat.

Follow the instructions for chopping and mincing but continue to process until the ingredients are puréed.

grate cheese.

This will produce a different texture than the grating disc but it has the advantage of controlling the degree of fineness. Cut the cheese into rough 2½ cm (1 in) cubes and process 1½-2 cups at a time.

make breadcrumbs of any texture from fine to rough.

Cut bread into 2½ cm (1 in) rough cubes and process 2 cups at a time.

grind nuts roughly in 2-3 seconds.

Making a nut paste will take a little longer. Some slippery nuts, such as sesame seeds will require a spoonful of water, otherwise they will rotate at the speed of the blade. Process about 1 cup at a time.

cream butter for sweet creams or savoury butters.

Always start with the hardest ingredients first and add the softened butter last.

make dips and spreads.

Follow the instructions for creaming butter and when everything is mixed, add the liquid ingredients, e.g. lemon juice.

| | make | all sauces. Hot, cold, white, brown and egg sauces. Very useful for breaking down lumps in sauces. Process 1½-2 cups at a time. |
| | mix | the whole range of ingredients from dry to liquid. |

Plastic Mixing Blade

2. The plastic mixing blade must not be used for the cutting of any solid ingredients and should be reserved to:

	mix	liquids.
	make	milkshakes and fruit drinks.
	beat	egg whites lightly, but will not beat them stiff as it will not aerate them sufficiently.
	whip	cream, but will produce a lesser volume than cream whipped with a whisk or beater.
	make	ice creams and sorbets.

Slicing Disc

3. The stainless steel slicing disc can only be used when pressing the ingredients with the plastic pusher through the feed tube, the slicing blades are available to produce slices of varying thickness. To ensure even, neat slices, cut the ingredients to fit the feed tube, and stack and arrange them there before processing.

The slicing disc will:

| | slice | French beans (arrange them horizontally in the feed tube), fruit for salads, preserves or flans. |
| | shred | cabbage for coleslaw. Cut the cabbage into pieces to fit the feed tube and press down with plastic pusher. |

Grating Disc

4. Stainless steel grating discs or shredders are available in varying grades. The ingredients which are to be grated must be pressed gently onto the disc.

The grating disc will:

| | grate | cheese (but hard cheeses should be grated with the steel blade), root vegetables and fruit, such as pears and apples, chocolate (which can also be processed with a steel blade). |
| | slice | cucumbers, zucchini, carrots, celery and similar vegetables (arrange them vertically and process while pressing them down with the plastic pusher). |

Useful Hints

All food processors are accompanied by an instruction booklet which should be studied in detail.

However, in the interest of safety and the greater enjoyment of the processor here are some of the points to remember.

Select the right attachment for the specific task, remembering that the steel blade will do most of the jobs, including those performed by the plastic blade.

Do not overload the processor, 1½-2 cups at a time will suffice. Cut solid ingredients into 2½ cm (1 in) rough cubes.

When combining ingredients of different textures, start with the hardest. By the time the softest is added, harder ingredients will be processed and mixed.

If some ingredients are very slippery, such as sesame seeds, add 1-2 tablespoons of liquid.

Always use the spatula to scrape down the bowl, the disc and the blades. Handle the blade with care. Wash it separately. Never take off the lid until the attachment has stopped rotating. Ice may be crushed, but make sure that the steel blade is in motion before dropping the ice through the feed tube.

When using the discs, always press the ingredients through the feed tube with the plastic pusher. However, do not press too hard.

Soups and Stocks

The processor finds many applications in the preparation of soups, from the chopping up of vegetables for the basic stocks to the processing of the many types and textures of ingredients which are used in soup recipes. Juliennes are no longer a chore and purées are a matter of seconds, slices are of an even thickness and flavours are perfectly blended. Having explored the recipes in this chapter, any others will seem easy and can be prepared applying the techniques learned here.

Clear Soups

Chicken Consommé with Chicken Quenelles

To obtain a clear, strongly flavoured Chicken Consommé use the recipe describing the Beef Consommé (page 10) and add 1 medium sized (no. 15) boiler chicken and a further 500 g (1lb) of giblets.
Cook for 2 hours instead of the 1½ hours shown in that recipe.

Serves 8

Makes 4 dozen small quenelles.

CHICKEN QUENELLES
Thanks to the food processor, the making of quenelles has been made easy. Provided the meat is well chilled before it is finely cut in the processor and before the cream is incorporated, at the speed at which the work is done there is no need to place the mixing bowl in ice.

**500 g (1 lb) chicken meat,
    preferably breast) chilled
2 egg whites
500 ml (1 pint) fresh chilled cream
salt, pepper
½ teaspoon nutmeg
2 tablespoons of finely chopped
    parsley for garnish.**

● 1. Cut the chicken meat into small chunks and place into the work bowl 1½ cups at a time. Process until very finely minced.
2. Place finely minced chicken meat in the bowl of a mixer, add salt, pepper and nutmeg.
● 3. Commence beating at high speed with paddle attachment.
4. Add egg whites, one at a time and continue beating for 2 minutes.
5. Remove from mixing bowl, place in a container and refrigerate for at least 2 hours.
● 6. Return the meat to the mixing bowl, commence beating with paddle attachment at high speed and gradually add the chilled cream. Continue beating for 2 minutes. If an electric mixer is not available, the cream can be incorporated by beating the mixture, placed in a large plastic or metal bowl, with a wooden spoon. This is hard work as it is important, through vigorous beating, to make the mixture light.
7. To form the small quenelles, use two teaspoons dipped in hot water. With one spoon pick up a teaspoonful of mixture and with the other, form it into an almond shaped dumpling.
8. Float the quenelles on the surface of chicken stock lightly simmering in a shallow baking dish.
9. Poach for 6 minutes.
10. To serve chicken consommé, place 4 to 6 quenelles in each soup bowl and cover with the consommé. Garnish with finely chopped parsely.

Note: If not required immediately, the mixture can be stored, covered, in the refrigerator for up to 24 hours.

Consommé with Juliennes of Vegetables

A basic beef stock when enriched by added meat and vegetable flavours will produce this elegant consommé.

Makes 2 litres (4 pints)

CONSOMMÉ
750 g (1½ lb) lean shin beef
500 g (1 lb) chicken giblets
1 carrot
3 leeks, white portion only
2 egg whites, whisked lightly
2.5 litres (5 pints) beef stock (see page 18)
salt and black pepper

CONSOMMÉ
- 1. Cut the meat and the giblet into cubes, approximately 2.5 cm (1 in), and place into the work bowl, 1½ cups at a time. Process for about 10 seconds.
- 2. Chop the carrot and the leeks roughly into small pieces and place into work bowl, 2 cups at a time. Process until finely cut.
  3. Combine the meat, giblets and vegetables in a stock pot and add the beef stock.
  4. Add the whisked egg whites and bring slowly to the boil, stirring constantly. When it boils, reduce heat and simmer uncovered for 1½ hours. Season with salt and black pepper.
  5. Strain through a cheese cloth stretched over a colander.

JULIENNES
1 carrot
2 stalks celery
1 turnip
1 leek, white portion only
250 g (8 oz) fresh green peas

JULIENNES
- 1. Set julienne disc or shredder in place and feed the carrot, celery and turnip, stacked horizontally, into the feed tube and push through with the plastic pusher. Cut the leek by hand into thin slivers.
  2. Put the julienne vegetables into the consommé and cook gently for 10 minutes. Add the peas at the last moment. Season and serve steaming hot with a glass of dry sherry.

Fish Soup with Herbs and Sliced Vegetables

Serves 8

1 quantity of fish stock (page 18)
2 carrots
2 stalks of celery
1 leek, white portion only
6 lemon slices
500 g (1 lb) fish cut into cubes for garnish

- 1. Set slicing disc in place and stack the carrots, celery and leek into the feed tube. Push through with plastic pusher.
  2. Put the vegetables and sliced lemon into the fish stock and cook gently for 10 minutes.
  3. Add fish cubes and continue cooking gently for another 5 minutes.
  4. Season, garnish with chopped parsley and serve with thick slices of hot, crusty French bread.

Clockwise from top: Chicken Consommé (page 9), Cold Tomato Soup (page 16); Prawn Bisque (page 15); Cream of Mushroom Soup (page 14)

Consommé Alsacienne, with Profiteroles Stuffed with Chicken Liver Purée

A variation of the beef consommé described in the recipe (page 10) this dish is very appropriate for a formal dinner party. It also demonstrates the versatility of the food processor, which is used throughout the preparation.

CONSOMMÉ
Follow the recipe on page 10, and serve garnished with chopped parsley. The profiteroles can be served either on a separate side plate or floated in the consommé at the moment of serving.

For 16-20 small profiteroles

PROFITEROLES
1¼ cups water
90 g (3 oz) butter
  cut into small pieces
125 g (4 oz) plain flour, sifted
4 60 g eggs
1 extra egg, beaten with
  1 tablespoon water
  for glazing
1 teaspoon salt
¼ teaspoon pepper
¼ teaspoon nutmeg

PROFITEROLES (CHOUX PASTRY)
1. Preheat the oven to 200°C (400°)
2. In a saucepan combine the butter, water and salt. Bring to boil.
3. Add the flour all at once while stirring quickly with a wooden spoon.
4. Continue cooking and stirring vigorously for 2-3 minutes until the mixture leaves the sides and clings together.
● 5. Place the dough into the work bowl and process for 10 seconds.
● 6. Add the eggs, one at a time, making sure that each egg is absorbed before the next one is added.
7. The profiteroles can be formed with two spoons dipped in water but a piping bag with a plain nozzle will make it much easier.
8. Fill the piping bag and form 2½-3 cm (1-1¼ in) puffs spaced 5 cm (2 in) apart on a buttered baking tray. (Any left over dough may be stored in refrigerator for up to 2 days).
9. Using a pastry brush, glaze each puff with the egg-water mixture and flatten them slightly.
10. Place the tray in the pre-heated oven and bake for about 20 minutes or until the profiteroles are golden brown.
11. When baked, remove from oven. With a sharp knife slit open one side. Remove any unbaked dough. Return to switched off oven and permit to dry out.

CHICKEN LIVER PURÉE
1 small onion
50 g (1½ oz) butter
250 g (8 oz) chicken livers
salt, freshly ground black pepper
1 tablespoon fresh herbs
  (thyme and/or marjoram)
2 tablespoons brandy
2 tablespoons honey

CHICKEN LIVER PURÉE
● 1. Cut the onion into four, place in the work bowl and process until finely chopped.
2. Melt butter in a frying pan and sauté onions lightly.
3. Add the chicken livers, salt and pepper, sauté lightly making sure that the livers are still pink inside.
4. At the last moment add the herbs and the honey. Pour in the brandy and flame.
● 5. When the flame dies down place the contents of the frying pan, approximately 1½ cups at a time into the work bowl. Process until very fine in texture.
6. Permit to cool so that the purée becomes slightly firm.
7. Using a piping bag with a small diameter nozzle, fill the profiteroles with the chicken liver purée.
8. Serve with consommé as previously suggested.

Puréed Soups

Pea or Lentil Soup

The peas and lentils are interchangeable and will produce a heart-warming winter soup with a great smoky flavour.

Serves 12

500 g (1 lb) split green peas
  or lentils
2 litres (4 pints) water
2½ teaspoons salt
60 g (2 oz) smoked pork fat
  (Speck)
1 carrot
1 onion
2 stalks celery
1 leek, white part only
1 sprig of fresh herbs
  (thyme, marjoram)
1 bay leaf
12 peppercorns
1 kg (2 lb) smoked pork ribs
  or ham bones

1. Rinse the peas or the lentils under running water.
2. Soak them over night in 2 litres (4 pints) of water to which the salt has been added.
3. Dice the pork fat and melt in frying pan.
● 4. Roughly cut the carrot, onion, celery and leeks. Place in work bowl and process until finely cut.
5. Sauté the diced vegetables in the melted pork fat until they are light brown.
6. Add the sautéed vegetables to the water and soaked peas or lentils. Also add the herbs, the peppercorns and the smoked pork ribs or ham bones.
7. Cook over a medium heat for 2½-3 hours. Stir from time to time, especially in the early stages, to make sure that the peas or lentils do not stick.
8. When cooked the soup should have a purée-type texture, the peas and lentils should have partly broken up.
9. After scraping off any meat and returning it to the soup, discard the bones. You may serve the soup as it comes out of the saucepan or after removing the bones, purée the soup, 2 cups at a time, in the work bowl.
10. Season and serve with hot crusty French bread.

Lettuce or Watercress Purée

A very pleasant light soup suitable as an introduction to a substantial dinner party.

Serves 8

1 bunch of watercress
or
2 medium-sized lettuce
3 tablespoons butter
300 g (10 oz) potatoes, peeled
1½ litres (3 pints) beef stock (page
  18)
salt
freshly ground black pepper
1 cup sour cream

1. Chop the watercress or lettuce coursely, (save ½ cup for garnish).
2. Sauté for a few minutes in the butter
3. Cook the potatoes in the beef stock until soft.
4. Add the sautéed watercress or lettuce to the cooked potatoes and continue cooking for another 15 minutes.
● 5. Place in the work bowl, two cups at a time and process for some 20 seconds or until it has a fine texture.
● 6. To serve, season with salt and freshly ground black pepper and finish off with the sour cream, which should be whisked into the soup. Garnish with watercress or lettuce which has been finely chopped in the work bowl.

Purée of Carrot Soup

The method shown here is basically a vichyssoise base soup and can also be used successfully with cauliflower, broccoli, celery or turnips. In the recipe below substitute any of these for carrots and use the same quantity.

Serves 8

750 g (1½ lb) carrots
500 g (1 lb) potatoes, peeled and
   quartered
3 stalks celery
2 onions (or 3 leeks)
1½ litres (3 pints) beef stock
salt
freshly ground black pepper
1 sprig of fresh herbs
1 cup sour cream

- 1. Roughly chop the vegetables in the work bowl.
  2. In a stock pot combine all ingredients except the sour cream.
  3. Cook for 1 hour.
- 4. Place in the work bowl, two cups at a time and process until mixture has a fine texture.
  5. To serve, season and finish off with the sour cream which should be whisked into the soup.

Cream Soups

Cream of Dried Mushroom Soup

A Central European version, using dried "Steinpilz" (yellow bolletus) to produce a very aromatic soup, garnished with fresh rosemary and button mushrooms.

Serves 8

60 g (2 oz) dried mushrooms
   (yellow bolletus)
500 g (1 lb) fresh mushrooms,
   save 8 small caps for garnish
3 tablespoons butter
3 tablespoons flour
1½ litres (3 pints) chicken stock
½ cup dry sherry
1 cup sour cream
salt
freshly ground black pepper
1 tablespoon fresh rosemary,
   finely chopped for garnish

- 1. In work bowl chop fresh and dried mushrooms (stalks and caps).
  2. Melt the butter in a large saucepan, add the mushrooms, cook for 5 minutes.
  3. Add the flour and cook for further 5 minutes.
  4. Gradually add the heated stock and simmer for ½ hour.
- 5. Place in the work bowl, 2 cups at a time and process until fine in texture.
  6. Strain through sieve.
  7. Return to saucepan, heat but do not boil, add cream and dry sherry, season with salt and freshly ground black pepper.
  8. Serve with one mushroom cap in each soup bowl and sprinkled with the rosemary.

Oyster Soup

A rather extravagant soup but the expense is well worthwhile.

Serves 8

3 dozen oysters (plus their water)
2 dozen additional oysters for garnish
2 litres (4 pints) fish stock (page 18)
1 teaspoon lemon zest, grated (the yellow of the skin)
1 sprig of fresh herbs (thyme or marjoram)
juice of one lemon
1 cup fresh cream
salt
freshly ground black pepper
2 tablespoons dill, finely chopped

1. Pour the fish stock into a stockpot, add all the ingredients except the oysters, the cream and the dill. Boil for 15 minutes.
2. Add 3 dozen oysters and simmer for 5 minutes.
● 3. Place in the work bowl, two cups at a time and process until fine in texture.
4. Strain through a fine sieve.
5. Add the cream, season and serve garnished with the remaining oysters and sprinkled with dill.

Bisque of Crayfish or Prawns

Ideally the crayfish should be live or the prawns uncooked. This is a regal dish and the special effort is well rewarded. If crayfish is unavailable, king prawns or crayfish shells and prawn shells can be substituted together with diced white fish.

Serves 6

1.5 kg (3 lb) crayfish or king prawns (or their shells)
1 carrot
1 large onion
1 sprig of fresh herbs (thyme, oregano or tarragon)
salt
freshly ground black pepper
100 g (3½ oz) rice
5 fresh tomatoes, peeled
1 tablespoon tomato purée
60 g (2 oz) butter
½ cup fresh cream
½ cup brandy (cognac if available)
1½ cups dry white wine
2 litres (4 pints) fish stock
¼ teaspoon cayenne pepper

● 1. In work bowl roughly chop the carrot, onion and herbs.
2. Sauté in the butter.
3. If using whole crayfish, split the crayfish into halves, remove the coral, the creamy parts and the liquid, squeeze through a sieve and reserve.
4. Add the split crayfish (or fresh prawns or crayfish shells or prawn shells) to the vegetables, season and cook slowly until they turn red (approximately 5-10 minutes).
● 5. Flame with cognac, add the white wine, the fish stock, the fresh tomatoes (previously chopped in processor) and the tomato purée. Season and cook covered for 20 minutes.
6. Remove the crayfish tails or prawns, take out the flesh and save. Return the shells to pot, add the rice and cook for 30 minutes.
● 7. Place all the contents of the pot, including the shells, 2 cups at a time in the work bowl and process for 20 seconds.
8. Strain through a medium sieve.
9. If using crayfish add the previously sieved internal parts.
10. Add the cream and the cayenne pepper. If necessary adjust the seasoning.
11. Cut the flesh of the crayfish tails or the prawns into large dice and add to the bisque or add diced white fish. Serve with a chilled Chablis-type wine.

Cold Soups

Tomato Soup with Fresh Basil

Serves 6

4 fresh tomatoes
1 onion
2 stalks of celery
1 carrot
1 leek, white part only.
1 clove garlic
60 g (2 oz) butter
1 bay leaf
6 peppercorns
1 tablespoon tomato paste
1½ litres (3 pints) beef stock (page 18)
salt
1 bunch of fresh basil

● 1. In the work bowl finely chop the onion, celery, carrot, leek and garlic.
2. In a large saucepan melt the butter and lightly sauté the finely cut vegetables.
● 3. Immerse the tomatoes in boiling water, peel them and chop them in the work bowl.
4. Add chopped tomatoes to the saucepan together with the bay leaf, peppercorns, tomato paste and beef stock. Season with salt and freshly ground black pepper. Cook for 30 minutes.
● 5. After 20 minutes of cooking, add the basil leaves and stalks which have been finely chopped in the work bowl (save some leaves for garnish) Cook for the remaining 10 minutes.
● 6. Place in the work bowl, 2 cups at a time, and process until fine in texture.
7. Strain through a fine sieve.
8. Refrigerate until serving. Garnish with a basil leaf.

Polish Cucumber Soup

A refreshing summer soup, its tangy flavour makes it a very good starter to summer dinners. It is important to use naturally preserved sour cucumbers, those pickled with vinegar are unsuitable.

Serves 8

2 tablespoons butter
3 sour dill cucumbers
2 cups cucumber brine
1 litre (2 pints) beef stock
1 cup sour cream
1 tablespoon plain flour
salt
freshly ground black pepper
2 lamb kidneys
1 tablespoon chives, finely chopped

● 1. Peel the cucumbers, stack them in the feed tube of the processor and press them down onto the slicing blade with the plastic pusher.
2. In a saucepan melt the butter and lightly sauté the sliced cucumbers, add the beef stock and cucumber brine and bring to boil.
3. Mix the flour into the cream and while stirring with a spoon add to the soup.
4. Taste carefully before seasoning as the brine may be quite salty.
● 5. In the work bowl chop the kidney and add to the soup while it is still simmering.
6. Serve chilled, garnished with chopped chives.

Cold Pipi Bisque

Prepared in the following manner, the pipis have a flavour and light green colour similar to the taoroah from New Zealand. Do not worry about the presence of some sand during the preparation, it will be removed during the sieving and what is left will sink to the bottom of the saucepan.

Serves 6

1 kg (2 lb) pipis
4 cups fish stock (page 18)
1 cup dry white wine
⅛ teaspoon tabasco sauce
salt
1 cup sour cream
juice of half a lemon
1 tablespoon of chopped chives

1. Simmer the pipis in the fish stock and white wine until all shells have opened, but not longer than 5-8 minutes.
2. Take the pipis out of shells and return them to stock.
● 3. Place in the work bowl, 2 cups at a time and purée until very fine.
4. Strain through a fine sieve, add the tabasco sauce, sour cream and lemon juice, season.
5. Serve chilled, garnished with chopped chives.

Vichyssoise

Serves 6

2 tablespoons butter
5 large leeks, white portion only
3 shallots
1 large onion
500 g (1 lb) peeled potatoes
3 cups chicken stock
1½ teaspoons salt
¼ teaspoon white pepper
2 cups sour cream
2 tablespoons chives, finely
    chopped for garnish

1. In a saucepan melt the butter.
● 2. Chop the leeks, shallots, onion and potatoes in the work bowl.
3. Add to the saucepan and sauté for about 10 minutes until golden brown.
4. Add all other ingredients except sour cream and chives.
5. Simmer for 45 minutes.
● 6. Place into the work bowl, 2 cups at a time and process until very fine in texture.
7. Return to saucepan, heat and add the cream.
8. Chill in refrigerator, check seasoning, serve cold sprinkled with the chives.

Avocado Soup

Serves 6

1 litre (2 pints) chicken stock
1 onion
½ garlic clove
2 ripe large avocados
juice of 1 lemon
1 cup sour cream
1 teaspoon dill, finely chopped
salt
black pepper

● 1. Chop the onions and the garlic in the work bowl.
2. In a saucepan combine the stock and the chopped onions and garlic. Cook for 10 minutes.
● 3. Cut the avocados in half, remove the seed and scrape the flesh into the work bowl, purée with the lemon juice and a cup of stock.
4. Add to the stock, stir in the cream, season and simmer for 2-3 minutes.
5. Place in the work bowl and process for 10 seconds. Strain through a sieve and refrigerate.
6. Serve chilled, garnished with chopped dill.

Stocks

Beef Stock

Makes 1½-2 litres(3·4 pints)

1½ kg (3 lb) shin beef
1 pig's trotter
1 veal knuckle
2 kg (4 lbs) beef bones (marrow
 bones if possible)
2 carrots
2 onions
2 leeks
4 stalks celery
1 tablespoon mixed dried herbs
1 bay leaf
6 sprigs parsley
2 cloves

1. Place the meat and the bones in a large saucepan and cover with cold water.
2. Bring the water to the boil and simmer for 5-10 minutes. Remove the scum which accumulates on the surface.
● 3. In the work bowl roughly chop the vegetables and add, together with all other ingredients, to the saucepan.
4. Add water to cover the ingredients by 2½ cm (1 in)
5. Simmer for 4-5 hours (do not boil) skimming occasionally.

Chicken Stock

To make Chicken Stock add 1 boiled chicken to the recipe for Beef Stock.

Fish Stock

Any white fish, fishbones and preferably fish heads can be used.

1.5 litres (3 pints) water
500 ml (1 pint) dry white wine
1 kg (2 lb) fish bones (and heads
 if possible)
2 large onions
½ cup parsley
2 carrots
250 g (½ lb) mushrooms
12 peppercorns
3 bay leaves
1 sprig each of thyme and
 marjoram
juice and zest of ½ lemon
salt and black pepper

1. In a stock pot combine the fish bones, the water and the white wine and bring to the boil
● 2. In the meantime, roughly chop vegetables and herbs. Place into the work bowl 2 cups at a time and process until finely cut.
3. Add the vegetables, herb mixture and the rest of the ingredients to the stock pot.
4. Boil slowly for 30 minutes, skim and when completed strain through cheese cloth stretched over a colander.

Clockwise from top: Pipi Sauce (page 27); Brown Mushroom Sauce (page 26); Aurora Sauce (page 24); Mayonnaise (page 21).

Sauces

No more lumpy sauces, broken down mayonnaise or curdled Hollandaise, the texture and consistency will always be right without fail. In many of the sauces no flour will be needed as the vegetable purée will provide a healthy thickening.

The seasoned butters shown here will give variety to savouries and sandwiches

Cold Sauces

Hollandaise Sauce

The following is the basic and thanks to the processor, disasterproof, recipe.

250 g (½ lb) butter
3 egg yolks
juice of ½ lemon
¼ teaspoon salt
⅛ teaspoon white pepper

1. Melt the butter and continue cooking until the milky parts have separated off. Use only the clear butter fat for the sauce.
● 2. Place egg yolks in work bowl and process for 20 seconds.
● 3. Through the feed tube, add the lemon juice, process for 5 seconds.
● 4. Continue to run the processor and through the feed tube slowly pour in the melted butter.
● 5. Add the salt and pepper and run the processor for a further 3 seconds.

Hollandaise Sauce Variations

HOLLANDAISE WITH BEATEN EGG WHITES
Stiffly whisk 2-3 egg whites and fold into the Hollandaise Sauce. This will produce a very light and elegant sauce for use with poached eggs, fish, fresh asparagus, etc.

SAUCE MOUSSELINE SABAYON
In the basic recipe add ½ cup fresh cream and ¼ cup dry white wine to the egg yolks. If you feel extravagant, use champagne instead of wine. Ideal for fish mousse or soufflé or steamed asparagus.

BERNAISE SAUCE
This sauce is actually Hollandaise Sauce to which a dry white wine is added.

Hollandaise Sauce (page 20)
3 shallots
½ cup dry white wine
2 tablespoons tarragon vinegar
1 tablespoon fresh or dried tarragon
½ tablespoon each fresh or dried thyme and marjoram (optional)
½ teaspoon freshly ground black pepper

● 1. Chop shallots in the work bowl.
2. In a saucepan combine the shallots, the wine, the vinegar, the herbs and the pepper.
3. Cook rapidly until a tablespoon of liquid is left.
● 4. Strain the liquid into the Hollandaise Sauce and run the processor for 3 seconds.

Mayonnaise

It is almost impossible to curdle mayonnaise in a processor. Should it happen, however, either add a few drops of vinegar before continuing adding the oil, or if this does not correct the mixture, take out the curdled sauce, rinse the work bowl, add a fresh egg yolk and gradually add the curdled mixture.

Basic Mayonnaise

Makes 1½ cups

2 egg yolks (at room temperature)
1¼ cups olive oil or vegetable oil
1 tablespoon French mustard
juice of 1 lemon
salt
freshly ground black pepper

- 1. Place the egg yolks and mustard in the work bowl and process for 10 seconds.
- 2. Pour in the oil, at first a few drops at a time, as the mayonnaise thickens it can be poured faster.
- 3. When all the oil is used, add the lemon juice, salt and pepper.

Mayonnaise Variations

MAYONNAISE WITH GREEN HERBS

To the mayonnaise add 3-4 tablespoons of a combination of all or any of the following green herbs which have been chopped in the work bowl: tarragon, chives, thyme, oregano, parsley, basil.

Use the Herb Mayonnaise in egg dishes with cold fish and meats and in hors d'oeuvres.

SAUCE RIVIERA, (GREEN MAYONNAISE WITH CREAM CHEESE, CAPERS, PICKLES AND ANCHOVIES)

To the mayonnaise add a paste made from:

125 g (4 oz) cream cheese
2 tablespoons each of capers and
  pickles
6 anchovy fillets
1 golden beet leaf
1 shallot
3 parsley leaves
1 tablespoon of any green herb
  available

- 1. Combine all ingredients in work bowl and process until they form a smooth paste.

SAUCE TARTARE

Normally Sauce Tartare would be made with hard boiled egg yolks, but in this recipe use the basic mayonnaise to which the following ingredients, chopped fine in the work bowl, are added:

1 dill cucumber
3 tablespoons capers
1 sprig each of parsley, tarragon
  and thyme
4 tablespoons chives, chopped
2 anchovy fillets
2 tablespoons red capsicum,
  chopped

SAUCE AIOLI

This tasty garlic mayonnaise is the classic accompaniment to the Provençal Fish Soup, bourride. It is also used with steamed fish, snails, boiled potatoes, French beans and hard boiled eggs.

1 thick slice of continental-type white bread, crust removed
3 tablespoons milk
4-8 garlic cloves (depending how strong a sauce is desired)
2 egg yolks
1¼ cup olive oil or vegetable oil
juice of one lemon
salt
freshly ground black pepper

1. Soak the bread in the milk for 10 minutes.
2. Squeeze the bread to remove as much of the milk as possible.
● 3. Place the bread and the garlic in the work bowl and process for some 15 seconds or until bread forms a paste.
● 4. Add the egg yolks and run for 10 seconds.
● 5. Continue running the processor and gradually add the oil.
● 6. Through the feed tube add the lemon juice, the salt and pepper. Mix for a few seconds.

Salad Dressings

Vinaigrette

The basic proportions for a vinaigrette of vinegar (or lemon juice) to oil are 1 to 3. However this can be varied to suit individual tastes.

Yield ½ cup

2 tablespoons white wine vinegar or lemon juice
6 tablespoons vegetable oil
½ teaspoon salt
1 teaspoon fresh mixed herbs
½ teaspoon French mustard

● 1. Combine all ingredients in work bowl and process for 10 seconds.

Vinaigrette Variations

VINAIGRETTE À LA CRÈME
Used for cold eggs, vegetables, and cold or hot fish

1 egg yolk
4 tablespoons cream or sour cream
½ cup vinaigrette (page 22)
juice of half lemon (if needed)

● 1. Combine the egg yolk and the cream in the work bowl and process for about 10 seconds.
● 2. Add vinaigrette a few drops at a time at first. As the mixture thickens the vinaigrette can be poured more quickly.
● 3. If necessary add more lemon juice, check and if necessary adjust seasoning.

VINAIGRETTE ROQUEFORT
A very tasty dressing for salads.

2 tablespoons Roquefort cheese (or any blue vein cheese)
2 tablespoons sour cream
½ cup vinaigrette (page 22)

● 1. Combine the cheese and the sour cream in the work bowl and process for 10 seconds.
2. Gradually add the vinaigrette.
3. If necessary adjust seasoning.

White Sauces

All white sauces are derived from two basic sauces, Béchamel and Velouté, their preparation is identical except that the first one is made with milk and the second with stock, either beef, chicken or fish stock. In both cases the roux, a mixture of flour and butter which becomes the binding agent, is the common element. It's worth remembering that the proportions of flour and butter should be about the same, and that a roux made from 50 g (1½ oz) flour is capable of binding 2½ cups of liquid.

In the variations, the Béchamel and the Velouté are interchangeable.

Béchamel Sauce

Yield 2½ cups

2½ cups milk
½ onion
1 sprig each of parsley and thyme
2 bay leaves
6 peppercorns
50 g (1½ oz) butter
50 g (1½ oz) plain flour
salt

● 1. In the work bowl chop the onion and herbs.
   2. Add the onion, herbs, peppercorns and bay leaves to the milk and heat gently for 10 minutes but do not boil. Strain.
   3. In a saucepan melt the butter and add the flour all at once, stirring constantly with a wooden spoon. If using an enamelled saucepan a wire whisk may be used. Stirring constantly, cook for 3-4 minutes until the roux turns a light blond colour.
● 4. Place the roux in the work bowl and with the processor running, add the strained milk through the feed tube. Continue processing until the sauce is smooth.
   5. Return the sauce to the saucepan and stirring periodically cook for some 15 minutes over a low heat until the sauce is smooth. The right degree of thickness can be achieved by either adding more milk to thin, or cooking longer to thicken the sauce.

Velouté Sauce

Yield 2½ cups

2½ cups stock, (beef, chicken, or fish)
50 g (1½ oz) butter
50 g (1½ oz) flour
salt
freshly ground black pepper

   1. In a saucepan melt the butter and add the flour all at once stirring constantly with a wooden spoon. If using an enamelled saucepan a wire whisk may be used. Stirring constantly, cook for 3-4 minutes until the roux turns a light blond colour.
● 2. Place the roux in the work bowl and with the processor running, add the heated stock through the feed tube. Continue processing until the sauce is smooth.
   3. Return the sauce to the saucepan and cook for 1-1½ hours over a low heat. If necessary skim the sauce from time to time. Season to taste.

Béchamel and Velouté Variations

CREAM SAUCE
For gratinéed dishes, vegetables, eggs, fish, poultry.

After cooking the sauce according to the basic recipe, return to the processor and while running it, add:

¾ cup fresh cream
juice of one lemon

SAUCE PARISIENNE
For eggs, fish, poultry and hot hors d'oeuvres.
After cooking the sauce according to the basic recipe, return to the processor and while running it, add:
¾ cup fresh cream
2 egg yolks

SAUCE AURORA
For eggs, fish, chicken and vegetables.

To the Cream Sauce (above) add:

3-4 tablespoons of tomato purée
(The amount depends on degree of colour and flavour required).

MORNAY SAUCE
For gratinéed dishes, eggs vegetables, poultry, veal and pastas.

After cooking the sauce according to the basic recipe, return to the processor and while running it, add:

50 g - 75 g (2 - 2½ oz) Swiss-type
cheese or parmesan, coarsely
grated
⅛ teaspoon nutmeg
⅛ teaspoon cayenne pepper
30 g (1 oz) butter

ONION SAUCE (SAUCE SOUBISE)
For eggs, veal, chicken, turkey, lamb, veal, vegetables and gratinéed dishes.

4 onions
¾ cup cream
⅛ teaspoon nutmeg

- 1. In the work bowl chop the onions.
  2. Add to the basic sauce and cook slowly for 15 minutes.
- 3. Return to the work bowl and process for 10 seconds.
  4. Strain through a fine sieve and return to saucepan.
  5. Finish off with cream, add the nutmeg and if necessary, adjust the seasoning.

Brown Sauces

This may not be the place to try to create a classical French brown sauce, the Espagnole. If prepared in the traditional manner, it requires first class ingredients and a great deal of time, some 20 hours of cooking!

Brown Sauce

Yield 4 cups

2 carrots
1 large onion
2 stalks of celery
3 sprigs parsley
1 sprig each of thyme and marjoram
5 tablespoons butter, pork fat or cooking oil
60 g (2 oz) plain flour
2 litres (3 pints) beef stock (page 18)
2 tablespoons tomato paste
2 bay leaves
6 peppercorns

1. In the work bowl chop the vegetables and the herbs.
2. In a large saucepan melt the butter (or pork fat or cooking oil).
3. Add the chopped vegetable-herb mixture and sauté slowly for 10 minutes.
4. Add the flour and stir constantly over moderate heat for further 10 minutes or until the flour turns nut-brown.
5. Add the hot stock and tomato paste.
6. Simmer slowly for 2-3 hours, skimming the fat and scum which rises to the surface.
7. At this stage there are two ways of dealing with the sauce, you may either just strain it or you may return it to the work bowl, 2 cups at a time, process for 10 seconds and then strain it. The result will be a thicker, purée-like sauce which may require thinning down with additional stock.
8. In both cases, correct the seasoning. If the sauce is not used immediately, cover it with plastic film and refrigerate or deep freeze.

Brown Sauce Variations

Whenever possible add any pan or cooking juices from the dishes which the sauces accompany. This will give the sauces added flavour.

SAUCE PIQUANTE
For pork dishes, fresh and smoked tongue, boiled beef.

To 2 cups of Brown Sauce add:

2 tablespoons pickles
2 tablespoons capers

1. Chop in the work bowl before adding to the sauce.

BROWN MUSTARD SAUCE (SAUCE ROBERT)
For turkey, pork dishes, smoked ham, hamburger, grilled meat.

To 2 cups of thick Brown Sauce add:

1 cup dry white wine
4 tablespoons of French mustard

1. Add the white wine first and simmer for 5 minutes, then place in work bowl, add the mustard and process for 5 seconds. Do not boil again.

BROWN MUSHROOM SAUCE (SAUCE DUXELLES)

For grilled or sautéed chicken, veal, beef, egg dishes and pasta.

2 cups Brown Sauce
125 g (4 oz) mushrooms
2 shallots
1 small onion
15 g (½ oz) butter
¼ cup dry vermouth
2 tablespoons tomato paste
2 sprigs parsley, chopped
salt
freshly ground black pepper

● 1. In work bowl chop the mushrooms, the shallots and the onion.
2. In a saucepan melt the butter and sauté the chopped vegetables for 5 minutes.
3. Add the wine and cook until the mixture is almost dry.
4. Add the tomato paste and the parsley.
5. Combine it with the Brown Sauce and season with salt and freshly ground black pepper.

Various Sauces

Greek Egg-Lemon Sauce

For fish, but sometimes served with meat or chicken.

30 g (1 oz) butter
2 tablespoons plain flour
1¼ cups fish, beef or chicken
    stock (depending on the type of
    dish with which it is served)
2 eggs
juice of 2 lemons
2 tablespoons cold water

1. Melt the butter in a saucepan with the flour to make a blond roux.
● 2. Place the roux in the work bowl and while processing add the hot stock. Work until smooth.
3. Return to the saucepan. Cook the sauce for 5 minutes.
● 4. Return to work bowl and while processing add the lightly beaten eggs, lemon juice and water.
5. Return to the pan and heat, but do not boil as this will cause the sauce to curdle.

Swiss Beer Sauce

1 onion
1 clove garlic
15 g (½ oz) butter
2½ cups beer
1 teaspoon vinegar
1 teaspoon brown sugar
1 bayleaf
salt
freshly ground black pepper
¼ teaspoon cinnamon
2 tablespoons potato flour (or
    cornflour)

● 1. In the work bowl chop the onion and the garlic.
2. Sauté them in a saucepan.
3. Add all the other ingredients except the potato flour.
4. Simmer for 15 minutes.
● 5. Pour into the work bowl and process for 5 seconds.
6. Strain through a fine sieve, back into the saucepan.
7. Mix the potato flour with a small quantity of water and thicken the sauce to the desired consistency.

Brown Bread Sauce

For game, roast lamb and roast chicken.

125 g (¼ lb) fine brown bread
   crumbs
½ litre (1 pint) milk
1 onion
6 cloves
1 teaspoon salt
⅛ teaspoon cayenne pepper
60 g (2 oz) butter
60 g (2 oz) coarse brown
   breadcrumbs

● 1. In the work bowl make the two lots of breadcrumbs.
   2. In a double saucepan cook the fine breadcrumbs, the milk
      and the onion, stuck with cloves, for ½ hour.
   3. Remove the onion and add the salt and the cayenne and
      half of the butter.
   4. In the remaining butter fry the coarse breadcrumbs until
      crisp and sprinkle over the sauce.

Russian Walnut Sauce

For steamed or fried fish.

20 fresh walnuts
1 teaspoon French mustard
2 egg yolks, hard boiled
1 tablespoon fine breadcrumbs
1 tablespoon oil
½ cup vinegar (or ¼ cup vinegar
   and juice of 1 lemon)
salt
freshly ground black pepper

● 1. In work bowl combine all ingredients, season, and process
      until very fine in texture. If too thick, add some water.

Pipi Sauce

For fish, quenelles, or fish mousse.

500 g (1 lb) pipis
500 ml (1 pint) fish stock (page 18)
60 g (2 oz) plain flour
juice of ½ lemon
salt
⅛ teaspoon cayenne pepper

   1. Gently simmer the pipis in the fish stock until they open.
   2. Take the pipis out of the shells and set aside.
   3. Melt the butter in a saucepan and blend in the flour to
      make a roux.
● 4. Place the roux in the work bowl and while processing add
      the hot stock. Work until smooth.
   5. Return to the saucepan and cook the sauce for 5 minutes.
   6. Add the pipis, and lemon juice and season with salt and
      cayenne pepper. Cook for another 5 minutes.
● 7. Place in the work bowl and process until smooth.
   8. Strain through a sieve and serve.

Seasoned Butters

Seasoned butters of many flavours are very versatile and can be used on hot dishes such as grills and fish, for basting of meat and fish dishes and while roasting or grilling. They can also be stirred into sauces or soups just before serving, to enrich their flavour and for decorating savouries and canapés if applied in a soft form from a piping bag.

- 1. Soft butter must be used and can easily be creamed in the work bowl.
- 2. The various flavourings are added while the butter is being creamed and the processor is run for a further 5-10 seconds to incorporate the flavourings.
- 3. Wrap in a long roll 3 cm (1¼ in) diameter in aluminium foil, refrigerate, and cut into slices as required.

The following variations are shown for 125 g (4 oz) of creamed butter:

MUSTARD BUTTER
For ham, smoked tongue, steaks.

2 tablespoons French mustard
2 tablespoons fresh herbs or parsley

ANCHOVY BUTTER
For fish, eggs, savouries, sauces.

6 anchovy fillets
juice of ½ lemon
2 tablespoons parsley

PARSLEY BUTTER (MAITRE d'HOTEL)
For steaks, fish, canapés.

4 tablespoons chopped parsley
juice of 1 lemon
freshly ground black pepper

TARRAGON BUTTER WITH MEAT FLAVOURING (SAUCE COLBERT)
For grilled meat and fish.

4 tablespoons chopped tarragon
2 tablespoons chopped parsley
salt
freshly ground black pepper
2 tablespoons melted meat glaze
  (meat stock reduced to a syrup)

SHALLOT BUTTER AND WHITE WINE
For steaks, hamburgers and enrichment of Brown Sauces.

2 shallots
¼ cup white wine
1 tablespoon melted meat glaze
salt
freshly ground black pepper

SHELLFISH BUTTER (PRAWN, CRAYFISH OR CRAB)
For sandwich spreads, hard boiled eggs, decoration of buffet dishes and for enrichment of sauces and soups.

125 g (4 oz) shellfish flesh
1½ tablespoons tomato paste
juice of ½ lemon
salt
freshly ground black pepper

Stuffings

An inventive cook will find a great deal of inspiration from the examples given here.

Not only can the stuffings be used in various meats but also in pancakes, filo pastry, vol-au-vents or pies.

The processor lends itself particularly well to the preparation of all types of stuffings for meats, poultry, vegetables and terrines. The following recipes do not represent a complete list but are meant to serve as an inspiration for the cook's unlimited imagination. The quantities of the stuffings are for approximately 1½-2 kg (3-4 lb) of meat.

Prune or Apricot Stuffing

A superb stuffing for roast pork.

2 onions
2 stalks celery
2 sprigs fresh herbs
½ clove garlic
15 g (½ oz) butter
juice of ½ lemon
1 tablespoon honey
1 cup pitted prunes or apricots
   which have been soaked in
   water for 1 hour
½ cup breadcrumbs
salt
freshly ground black pepper

● 1. Chop the onions, celery and garlic in the work bowl.
   2. Melt the butter in a saucepan and lightly sauté the chopped vegetables and garlic.
   3. Add the remaining ingredients and cook for 5 minutes.
● 4. Return to work bowl and process for 10 seconds.

Brain Stuffing

An excellent filling for pancakes, or delicious wrapped in filo pastry, baked and served as an hors d'oeuvre.

Yield 2 cups

3 shallots
2 sprigs of thyme
15 g (½ oz) butter
3 lamb brains
1 litre (2 pints) water
1 tablespoon white vinegar
½ cup sour cream
½ cup breadcrumbs
juice of ½ lemon
salt
freshly ground black pepper

● 1. Chop the shallots and thyme in the work bowl.
   2. Sauté them lightly in melted butter in a frying pan.
   3. In a saucepan, boil the water, add some salt and the vinegar, place the brains in the water and blanch for 5 minutes.
● 4. Roughly cut up the brains, place in work bowl, add remaining ingredients and process for 10 seconds. Season to taste.

Apple and Sausage Stuffing

Adds extra piquancy to roast duckling.

250 g (½ lb) pork sausages
5 Granny Smith apples, peeled,
 cored and quartered
1 tablespoon honey
¼ teaspoon cinnamon
¼ teaspoon salt
4 leaves of fresh sage
3 tablespoons brandy
½ cup port
½ cup beef stock
freshly ground black pepper

1. Sauté the sausages in oil in a frying pan until light brown. Chop into chunks and set aside.
2. Sauté the apples in the sausage fat until light brown. Set aside.
3. Drain off the sausage fat and in the frying pan reduce the port and the beef stock to 2-3 tablespoons.
● 4. Combine all ingredients in the work bowl and process until coarse in texture (approximately 10 seconds).

Pea and Mint Stuffing

Delicious with stuffed boned loin of lamb.

2 cups frozen peas
1 litre (2 pints) water
2 sprigs of mint
1 clove garlic
½ cup breadcrumbs
salt
freshly ground black pepper

1. Bring the peas to the boil. Strain.
● 2. Place all ingredients in the work bowl and process for 10-15 seconds.

Herb and Giblet Stuffing

A tasty accompaniment to roast chicken.

2 shallots
1 onion
2 sprigs parsley
1 sprig each tarragon and thyme
30 g (1 oz) butter
250 g (8 oz) chicken giblets (heart,
 liver, gizzard)
½ cup freshly cut breadcrumbs
½ cup cream (or cottage) cheese
⅛ teaspoon salt
freshly ground black pepper
juice of 1 lemon

● 1. Chop the shallots, onion, parsley and herbs in the work bowl.
2. Sauté them lightly in melted butter in a saucepan.
3. Add the giblets and sauté for 5 minutes.
● 4. Place the giblets into the work bowl and process until coarse in texture.
5. Add all other ingredients and process for 10 seconds.

Mushroom and Goose Liver Stuffing

½ kg (1 lb) mushrooms
2 shallots
50 g (1½ oz) butter
200 g (7 oz) goose livers (or
    chicken livers)
½ cup Madeira or port
1 sprig of thyme
¼ teaspoon mixed spices
salt
freshly ground black pepper

● 1. In the work bowl, chop the mushrooms and the shallots.
   2. In a saucepan, melt the butter and sauté the mushrooms
     and shallots.
   3. Add the goose or chicken livers and fry them for 2-3
     minutes, the livers should be pink inside.
● 4. Place all ingredients in the work bowl and process until
     fine in texture. Season to taste.

Olive and Minced Lamb Stuffing

125 g (4 oz) lean lamb
2 onions
1 cup breadcrumbs (freshly cut in
    the processor and soaked in
    some stock)
12 stoned black olives
1 egg
2 tablespoons chopped fresh
    herbs
¼ teaspoon mixed spices
1 clove garlic
salt
freshly ground black pepper

● 1. Cut lamb into chunks and mince in the work bowl.
● 2. Add remaining ingredients and work for 5-10 seconds to
    combine.

Rice and Kidney Stuffing

2 onions
1 stalk celery
30 g (1 oz) butter
½ cup chicken or beef stock
⅓ cup white rice
1 sprig fresh rosemary
½ clove garlic
¼ teaspoon mixed spices
4 lamb kidneys
salt
freshly ground black pepper

● 1. In the work bowl, chop the onions and celery.
   2. In a saucepan, melt the butter and sauté the chopped
     onions and celery.
   3. Add the rice and sauté for a further 3 minutes.
   4. Add the stock and simmer for 15 minutes by which time
     the liquid will be absorbed.
● 5. Place the rosemary, garlic, spices and lamb kidneys in the
     work bowl and chop to a fine texture.
   6. In a frying pan, melt some butter and sauté the kidney
     mixture for 2-3 minutes.
   7. Combine all ingredients, season and use according to
     meat recipe.

Entrées and Luncheon Dishes

Here the application and possibilities of the processor are endless. Each dish shows the versatility of the processor and permits the cook full reign of imagination.

Tarts and Quiches

Onion Tart with Anchovies and Black Olives

A pizza-type dish made in a tart shell. Other fillings may be invented.

Serves 6

1 20 cm (8 in) partly baked tart shell made with **Pâte Brisée** (page 79)
1 kg (2 lb) onions
4 tablespoons cooking oil
4 sprigs parsley
2 sprigs thyme
2 bay leaves
1 garlic clove
½ teaspoon salt
⅛ teaspoon powdered cloves
⅛ teaspoon freshly ground black pepper
8 fillets of anchovy
16 pitted black olives

1. Preheat the oven to 180°C (350°F).
● 2. In the work bowl, chop the onions, herbs and garlic.
3. Cook them very slowly in the oil for approximately 1 hour or until tender.
4. Add the salt, cloves and pepper, and mix well.
5. Spread the mixture in the pastry shell.
6. Decorate with the anchovy fillets and the black olives.
7. Bake in top part of the oven for 10-15 minutes.

Leek Quiche (Flamiche)

Serves 6

1 20 cm (8 in) partly baked tart shell made with **Pâte Brisée** (page 79)
½ kg (1 lb) leek, white part only
¾ cup water
2 teaspoons salt
60 g (2 oz) butter
3 eggs
1¼ cups fresh cream
⅛ teaspoon nutmeg
⅛ teaspoon freshly ground black pepper
30 g (1 oz) Swiss-type cheese, grated

1. Preheat the oven to 190°C (375°F).
● 2. Fit the slicing disc into the work bowl. Through the feed tube, press the leek on the slicing disc with the plastic pusher.
3. In a saucepan, cover the leeks with water to which the butter and some of the salt have been added and stew for 20 minutes.
4. Strain the leeks and spread them out on the pastry shell.
● 5. In the work bowl, using the steel blade, beat the eggs, cream and seasoning.
6. Pour into the pastry shell.
● 7. In the work bowl, using the grating disc, grate the cheese.
8. Sprinkle the cheese onto the tart and dot it with small pieces of butter.
9. Bake for 20-30 minutes until the egg-cream mixture sets and the surface is golden brown.

Classical Cheese Soufflé (page 42).

Oyster and Spinach Tart

This is a rather expensive dish, but it is filling and nourishing and served with a salad and some chilled white wine it is a meal in itself.

Serves 6

1 20 cm (8 in) baked tart shell made with Pâte Brisée (page 79)

3 shallots

30 g (1 oz) butter

250 g (½ lb) spinach or silverbeet leaves

½ teaspoon salt

⅛ teaspoon freshly ground black pepper

⅛ teaspoon nutmeg

3-6 dozen oysters (depending on how extravagant you wish to be)

2 eggs

1 cup fresh cream

30 g (1 oz) Swiss-type cheese, grated

1. Preheat the oven to 190°C (375°F).
2. Roughly chop the shallots and sauté lightly in the butter.
3. Add the spinach or silverbeet leaves and cook over moderate heat for 5 minutes.
4. Add the nutmeg and the seasoning.
● 5. Place in the work bowl and process until roughly cut.
6. Spread the spinach and shallots onto the pastry shell.
● 7. In the work bowl, using the steel blade, beat the eggs and cream and season with salt and black pepper.
8. Arrange the oysters on top of the spinach and pour the egg and cream mixture on top.
● 9. In the work bowl, using the grating disc, grate the cheese.
10. Sprinkle the cheese onto the tart and dot it with small pieces of butter.
11. Bake for 20-30 minutes, until the egg-cream mixture sets and the surface is golden brown.

Pies

Pies are very much part of English cooking and originated in the days before the potato was introduced, the pastry serving to mop up the juices. Various types of pastry may be used, for example puff pastry, short pastry or sweet pastry. Nowadays there is quality deep-frozen pastry available which makes the cooking of pies very easy. However, if you wish, use either the Pâte Brisée (page 79) or the Rough Puff pastry (page 79).

The recipes quoted here are for traditional English pies.

Shropshire Rabbit Pie

Serves 3-4

2 large onions

4 sprigs of thyme

1 rabbit, jointed and cut into cubes

2 tablespoons plain flour

250 g (½ lb) ham or bacon

60 g (2 oz) butter

1 litre (2 pints) beef stock

1 bay leaf

salt

freshly ground black pepper

250 g (8 oz) flaky or short pastry

1 egg mixed with 1 tablespoon water

1. Preheat oven to 200°C (400°F).
● 2. In the work bowl, chop the onions, thyme and ham or bacon.
3. Place in a saucepan and add the cubed, floured rabbit. Sauté in the butter until light brown.
4. Add the beef stock and bay leaf, season with salt and black pepper and simmer for 1 hour.
5. Allow to cool. Cover with a pastry lid, decorate with pastry trimmings. Glaze with the egg and water mix.
6. Bake for 30 minutes or until the crust is golden brown.

English Bacon Pie

This pie resembles the quiche except that it is eaten cold and is covered with a pastry lid.

Serves 6-8

1 large onion
30 g (1 oz) butter
6 rashers of bacon (rindless)
8 eggs
2 cups of fresh cream
⅛ teaspoon nutmeg
salt
freshly ground black pepper
500 g (1 lb) short pastry (page 79)

1. Preheat oven to 180°C (350°F).
● 2. In the work bowl, chop the onion.
3. In a frying pan sauté the onion lightly in the melted butter.
● 4. In the work bowl, chop the bacon roughly and then sauté lightly.
5. Combine the onions and the bacon.
● 6. In the work bowl, combine the eggs, cream, nutmeg, salt and pepper.
7. Place the ham and onion mix in a pie dish and pour the egg mix over it, (reserve a little egg mix for glazing).
8. Cover with a pastry lid, decorate with pastry trimmings cut into leaf and flower shapes. Glaze with egg mix.
9. Bake for approximately 45 minutes.
Allow to cool for several hours and serve cut into wedge shaped slices.

Variation: Mushrooms and parsley may be added to the bacon. Also the pie dish can be lined and baked blind before filling it with the ingredients and covering it with a lid.

Fish Pie

The fish pie can be made with a pastry lid or with a mashed potato topping. Virtually any filleted fish may be used.

Serves 4-6

500 g (1 lb) fish cut into 2½ cm
  (1 in) cubes
½ litre (1 pint) fish stock
  velouté (page 23)
2 onions
250 g (8 oz) short pastry (page 79)
1 egg mixed with 1 teaspoon
water

1. Preheat oven to 200°C (400°F).
● 2. In the work bowl, slice the onions with slicing disc.
3. In a pie dish, arrange in layers the fish cubes and sliced onions and seasoning.
4. Pour the velouté over the fish
5. Roll out pastry to make a lid. Cover the pie with the pastry.
6. Decorate with pastry trimmings and glaze with the egg and water mix.
7. Bake until the pastry is golden brown.

or

MASHED POTATO TOPPING
500 g (8 oz) potatoes
90 g (3 oz) butter
½ cup milk
salt
freshly ground black pepper
50 g (2 oz) Swiss-type cheese
1 tablespoon chives, chopped
1 egg mixed with 1 teaspoon
  water

or

MASHED POTATO TOPPING
● 1. Cook the potatoes and in work bowl with steel blade mash the potatoes, add some of the butter, the milk and season with salt and black pepper.
2. Cover the pie mixture with the mashed potatoes, sprinkle with the cheese, the chives and dot with small pieces of butter.
3. Bake until topping is golden brown.

Lamb and Apple Pie

Serves 6-7

2 stalks celery
3 onions
60 g (2 oz) butter
1 kg (2 lb) lamb cut into 2½ cm (1 in) cubes
1 litre (2 pints) water
2 cloves
4 sprigs fresh thyme
salt
freshly ground black pepper
1 tablespoon plain flour
1 kg (2 lb) Granny Smith apples
½ kg (1 lb), or sufficient to make a pie lid, of short pastry (page 79)
1 egg mixed with 1 tablespoon water

1. Preheat oven to 200°C (400°F).
● 2. In the work bowl, chop the celery and onions.
3. Place in a saucepan, add the lamb and sauté lightly in the butter.
4. Add the water, cloves and thyme and season.
5. Add the flour mixed with a little water and simmer slowly for 1½-2 hours. Allow to cool.
6. Peel, core and quarter the apples.
● 7. Fit the slicing disc in the work bowl, through the feed tube, press the apples onto the slicing disc with the plastic pusher.
8. Arrange the meat and the sliced apples in layers in a pie dish.
9. Cover with a pastry lid, decorate with pastry trimmings. Glaze with the egg and water mix.
10. Bake for 30 minutes or until the crust is golden brown.

Herb and Vegetable Pie

Originally a Lenten dish, this pie makes a tasty and filling meatless meal.

Serves 6-8

2 medium onions
4 sprigs parsley
2 sprigs each thyme and marjoram
1 tablespoon chives, chopped
750 g (1½ lb) short pastry (page 79)
250 g (½ lb) cooked new potatoes cut into 1 cm (½ in) cubes
1 kg (2 lb) mixed, fresh or frozen vegetables, cooked and cooled
4 eggs
1 extra egg mixed with 1 teaspoon water for glaze
2 cups fresh cream (milk may be substituted)
salt
freshly ground black pepper

● 1. Preheat oven to 200°C (400°F).
2. In the work bowl finely chop the onions, parsley and herbs.
3. Line the pie dish with pastry and reserve some for the lid.
4. Bake the lined pie dish, covered with foil, for 15 minutes. Allow to cool.
5. Place the vegetables in layers, sprinkled with the onion herb mixture and the seasoning, into the lined pie dish.
● 6. In the work bowl, mix the eggs and the cream (or milk). Pour into the vegetables. The mixture should cover the vegetables. If necessary add more egg and cream mixture. Put on the pastry lid, decorate with pastry trimmings shaped into leaves or flowers. Glaze with the egg and water mix.
7. Return to the oven and bake at 200°C (400°F) for 30 minutes or until the crust is golden brown.

Florentine Pancake "Cake" (page 43)

Gratins

Gratin of Ham, Onions, Eggs and Grated Potatoes

Serves 4

2 onions
2 tablespoons butter, melted
100 g (3 oz) ham
4 eggs
½ clove garlic
2 sprigs parsley
1 tablespoon chives, chopped
100 g (3 oz) Swiss-type cheese
½ cup fresh cream or milk
¼ teaspoon salt
freshly ground black pepper
3 medium-sized potatoes
15 g (½ oz) butter

1. Preheat oven to 190°C (375°F).
● 2. In the work bowl, chop the onions.
3. Sauté the onions in the melted butter until tender but not brown.
● 4. In the work bowl, chop the ham and add to the onions, sauté for 2 minutes.
● 5. Grate the cheese with the grating disc and combine it in the work bowl with all remaining ingredients except the potatoes and butter.
6. Add the sautéed ham and onions.
● 7. In the work bowl, through the feed tube and using the grating disc, grate the potatoes. Squeeze as much as possible of the liquid out of the grated potatoes and stir them into the mixture.
8. Butter a 5 cm (2 in) deep baking or gratin dish and pour in the mixture, dot with small pieces of butter.
9. Bake 30-40 minutes or until the top is golden brown.

Gratin of Vegetable Purée

Use cauliflower, broccoli, carrots, leeks, Brussels sprouts, onions.

Serves 6 to 8

¾-1 kg (1½-2 lb) vegetable of your choice
1 litre (2 pints) water
2 eggs
½ cup fresh cream
4 tablespoons butter
¼ teaspoon nutmeg
salt
freshly ground black pepper
½ cup Swiss-type or parmesan cheese

1. Preheat oven to 190°C (375°F).
2. Blanch the vegetables in boiling salt water for 3-5 minutes (depending on type of vegetable used).
3. Drain, cool and cut up into rough chunks.
● 4. In work bowl, combine the vegetables, eggs, cream, 2 tablespoons butter and the nutmeg. Process for 45 seconds or until puréed. Season with salt and black pepper.
5. Pour into a gratin dish.
● 6. Grate the cheese with the grating disc. Sprinkle on top of mixture and dot with small pieces of butter.
7. Bake 30-40 minutes or until the top is golden brown.
Note: The dish may be also placed under a preheated griller until the cheese turns brown.

Profiteroles and Gnocchi

Profiteroles filled with a variety of savoury stuffings and garnished with a number of tasty sauces can be served either as part of an elegant luncheon or they are a very pleasant way to start a dinner. The choux pastry from which they are made (page 12) is easy to prepare, and can be shaped into the desired size puff with either a piping bag or with the help of two tablespoons.

The following stuffings are only a suggestion and may serve as an inspiration for further creative preparations by the imaginative cook. The stuffings can also be used in savoury pancakes.

Sweetbread or Brain Stuffing with Pine Nuts

2 litres (4 pints) water
1 teaspoon salt
2 tablespoons white wine vinegar
3 lamb brains (or sweetbreads)
1 onion
½ clove garlic
1 tablespoon butter
2 sprigs each thyme and oregano
½ cup sour cream
juice of ½ lemon
½ cup roasted pine nuts
salt
freshly ground black pepper

1. Boil the water with the salt and vinegar, add the brains and blanch for 5 minutes. Strain the water.
● 2. In the work bowl finely chop the onion and the garlic.
3. Sauté the onion and the garlic until soft.
● 4. Roughly chop the brains and place in work bowl. Add all ingredients and process for 5 seconds.

Fish Mousse Stuffing Profiteroles with Fish Velouté Sauce

1 onion
1 carrot
2 stalks celery
6 peppercorns
1 bay leaf
1 teaspoon dried herbs
1.5 litres (3 pints) water
500 ml (1 pint) dry white wine
1 kg (2 lb) fillets of any fresh,
   white fleshed fish
½ cup cream
juice of one lemon
chives
salt
freshly ground black pepper
16-20 small profiteroles (page 12)

VELOUTÉ
juice of one lemon
⅛ teaspoon cayenne pepper

● 1. In work bowl chop the vegetables.
2. In large saucepan boil the vegetables, the peppercorns, the bay leaf and the herbs in 1½ litres (3 pints) water for 30 minutes. Add the white wine.
3. Add the fish fillets and simmer for ten minutes, strain and save the fish stock for velouté sauce (page 23).
● 4. Place the cooked fish fillets in the work bowl and process until fine in texture.
5. Add the cream, the lemon juice, the chives and season. Process for 5 seconds.
6. Place the stuffing inside the profiteroles, make a velouté sauce (page 23) with the fish stock, adding some lemon juice and cayenne pepper. Serve the sauce cold spooned over the puffs.

Prawn and Ginger with Cream Cheese

500 g (1 lb) prawns, cooked
250 g (½ lb) cream cheese or
   ricotta
½ cup fresh cream
juice of one lemon
salt
freshly ground black pepper
1 tablespoon preserved
   unsweetened ginger
1 teaspoon chives

1. Shell the prawns, remove the vein and chop roughly.
● 2. Place in work bowl and process until fine in texture.
● 3. Add all ingredients and process for a few seconds until they are combined.

Cheese Stuffing

500 g (1 lb) cream cheese (ricotta)
100 g (3½ oz) Roquefort or any
   blue vein cheese
½ cup sour cream
½ cup capers
salt
freshly ground black pepper

● 1. In the work bowl combine the two types of cheese, process for 5 seconds, add the sour cream, the capers and process for further 5 seconds.
Note: Be careful when seasoning, the cheese and the capers are already salty.

Potato Gnocchi with Cheese

Makes 12 gnocchi, 7.5 x 2.5 cm (3 x 1½ in)

3-4 potatoes, 500 g (1 lb)
200 g (7 oz) warm choux pastry
   (page 12)
125 g (4 oz) Swiss-type cheese or
   parmesan, grated in the
   processor
water
salt
freshly ground black pepper
½ cup Swiss or parmesan cheese,
   grated

1. Peel, quarter and boil the potatoes in salted water. Drain.
● 2. Place the potatoes in the work bowl and process 'until mashed, (2 cups at a time).
● 3. Add the choux pastry and 45 g (1½ oz) cheese and process until mixed. Season to taste.
4. With a tablespoon pick up the mixture, in your palm form circular flat pieces 6 cm (2½ in) in diameter and 2½ cm (1 in) high.
5. Place them in a shallow dish of gently simmering salted water and cook for 15-20 minutes. When done they should be approximately double the original size.
6. Drain them in a colander and serve them sprinkled with the remaining grated cheese.

A selection of dips (pages 46-7).

Soufflés

Classical Cheese Soufflé

Serves 6

4 cups Béchamel Sauce (page 23),
   (less for a thicker sauce) or
4 cups milk
3½ cups cheddar or Swiss-type
   cheese
¼ teaspoon nutmeg
10 eggs, separated
salt
freshly ground black pepper

1. Preheat oven to 190°C (375°F).
- 2. In the work bowl, grate the cheese and set aside.
- 3. Pour the egg yolks into the work bowl and process for 5 seconds.
4. When the Béchamel Sauce has cooled a little, add the egg yolks and stir with a wooden spoon until well mixed.
5. Add 3 cups of grated cheese and the nutmeg, stir in thoroughly.
6. In a mixing bowl, using either electrical or hand beater, whisk the egg whites, to which a pinch of salt has been added, until very stiff.
7. Slowly fold ¼ of the beaten egg whites into the sauce, then mix in the remainder.
8. Taste and season with salt and black pepper.
9. Butter either one large or 6 small soufflé dishes and gently pour in the mixture. Sprinkle with the remaining cheese.
10. For a more dramatic effect, with some string attach a paper collar to the large soufflé dish and fill the dish almost to the top.
11. Bake for 45 minutes. Serve with a green salad and a lightly chilled red wine.

Prawn Soufflé

Serves 6

250 g (½ lb) prawns, shelled and
   cooked for purée
125 g (¼ lb) prawns, cooked and
   diced
¾ cup thick Béchamel Sauce
   (page 23)
3 eggs, separated
¼ teaspoon nutmeg
salt
freshly ground black pepper

1. Preheat oven to 190°C (375°F).
2. In the work bowl, purée shelled, cooked prawns.
3. Combine puréed prawns with diced prawns and Béchamel Sauce.
4. In the work bowl, process egg yolks for 5 seconds.
5. Add egg yolks and nutmeg to Béchamel Sauce mixture.
6. In a mixing bowl, using an electric or hand beater, whisk egg whites and a pinch of salt until very stiff.
7. Slowly fold ¼ of the egg whites into the mixture. Then mix in remainder. Season to taste.
8. Butter 1 large or 6 small soufflé dishes and gently pour in the mixture.
9. Bake for approximately 45 minutes. Serve hot with salad and a chilled, dry white wine.

Pancakes and Crêpes

The various dishes made with pancakes are very versatile. As entrées, in pancake cakes (gâteau de crêpes) as main courses and in sweetened pancakes, they provide endless possibilities. For example any of the stuffings for profiteroles (pages 39-40) may be used as savoury pancake fillings.

Savoury Pancake Batter

Makes 12 pancakes, 15-16½ cm (6-6½ in)

250 g (½ lb) plain flour
4 eggs
2 cups milk
¼ teaspoon salt
4 tablespoons butter, melted
butter or oil for frying

1. In work bowl combine all ingredients and process for 10 seconds.
2. Pour into jug and let stand in refrigerator for 1 hour.
3. Heat the pancake pan and with pastry brush apply some melted butter or cooking oil.
4. With ladle pour some batter in the middle of the pan and tilt it to distribute the batter.
5. Use the first pancake to test the consistency of the batter, if too thick dilute with some water.
6. Use pallet knife to turn the pancake.

Note: Pancakes wrapped in plastic film will keep in a refrigerator for several days.

Florentine Pancake 'Cake'

Serves 6-8

24 cooked pancakes, 15-16½ cm
(6-6½ in)

SPINACH FILLING
3 shallots
30 g (1 oz) butter
375 g (¾ lb) spinach, blanched
¼ teaspoon salt
⅛ teaspoon nutmeg

CHEESE AND MUSHROOM FILLING
250 g (½ lb) mushrooms
3 shallots
15 g (½ oz) butter
500 g (1 lb) cream cheese (ricotta)
1 egg
2 cups mornay sauce (Béchamel
with cheese) (page 24)
3 tablespoons grated cheese
15 g (½ oz) butter
salt
freshly ground black pepper

1. Preheat oven to 180°C (350°F).
2. In the work bowl chop 3 shallots.
3. Lightly sauté the shallots in the butter.
4. In the work bowl combine the blanched spinach, the shallots, the salt, and the nutmeg. Process for 5 seconds. Set aside.
5. In the work bowl chop the mushrooms and shallots.
6. Sauté the mushrooms and the shallots for 5 minutes.
7. Place the cream cheese, the egg and ¾ cup of mornay sauce in the work bowl, add the mushrooms, season and process to combine.
8. Butter a round 23 cm (9 in) diameter soufflé dish. Cover the bottom of the dish with some cheese and mushroom filling. In the centre place a pancake, spread it with some spinach filling. Place alternating layers of pancakes and fillings, topping it with a pancake. Spread the remaining cheese sauce on top and on the sides of the mound. Sprinkle with 3 tablespoons of grated cheese and dot with pieces of butter.
9. Bake for 30 minutes or until the top is golden brown.

Potato Pancakes

1 onion
3 sprigs parsley
5 eggs
¼ teaspoon nutmeg
1 teaspoon salt
¼ teaspoon freshly ground black
  pepper
5 tablespoons plain flour
1 kg (2 lb) potatoes, peeled
cooking oil

Serves 6-8

● 1. In work bowl chop the onion and the parsley.
2. In a bowl lightly beat 5 eggs, add the seasoning and the flour and mix together.
● 3. In the work bowl, using the grating disc, grate the potatoes.
4. Using your hands squeeze as much water as possible out of potatoes.
5. Mix into the rest of ingredients.
6. In a frying pan preheat some oil and using a tablespoon form thin round pancakes 5-8 cm (2-3 in) in diameter. Fry until golden brown on both sides.
7. Serve as a vegetable with meats and poultry.

Note: The pancakes may be made about 15 cm (6 in) in diameter and can be made into a pancake cake similar to the one described on page 43.

Fritters

The two basic ways of making fritter batter can be used in any recipes where seafood, meat, fruit or vegetables are to be cooked and fried.

The second recipe will result in a fluffy and crisp casing.

Basic Fritter Batter 1

125 g (¼ lb) flour
1 egg
30 g (1 oz) melted butter
½-¾ cup half milk half water
⅛ teaspoon salt

● 1. Combine all ingredients in the work bowl and process until well mixed together.

Basic Fritter Batter 2

125 g (¼ lb) flour
1 egg yolk
30 g (1 oz) melted butter
⅛ teaspoon salt
½-¾ cup warm water
2 egg whites, stiffly whisked

● 1. In processor combine the flour, egg yolk, melted butter and the salt. Process to mix the ingredients together.
● 2. Add the warm water and process for 5 seconds. Allow to cool.
● 3. Whisk the egg whites and fold into mixture.
4. This batter is best fried or deep fried in very hot fat.

Top: Unmoulded Cold Salmon Mousse (page 47)
Bottom: Fish Mousse (page 48).

Dips

Macadamia Nut Dip

Serves 8-10

12 Macadamia nuts
4 shallots
2 tablespoons mixed pickles
6 stuffed olives
1 cup plain yoghurt
½ cup sour cream
¼ teaspoon salt
freshly ground black pepper
1 tablespoon chives, chopped
6 stuffed olives

● 1. Place nuts, shallots, pickles and olives into the work bowl and process for 5 seconds.
● 2. Add the yoghurt, the cream and seasonings and process for a further 5 seconds.
3. Place in a bowl and refrigerate, overnight if possible, this will permit flavours to blend.
4. To serve form a mound, sprinkle with the chopped chives and decorate with the stuffed olives.

Caviar Cream Cheese Dip

Serves 8-10

1 cup cream cheese (cottage)
½ cup plain yoghurt
3 sprigs of dill
juice of 1 lemon
salt
freshly ground black pepper
90 g (3 oz) red caviar (salmon roe)

● 1. Place all ingredients except the caviar in the work bowl and process for 5-8 seconds.
2. Transfer to a bowl and mix in most of the caviar, keeping 1 tablespoon for garnish.
3. Transfer on to a serving dish, form into a mound and garnish by sprinkling the remainder of the caviar over the dip. Refrigerate before serving.

Herring Cream Dip

Serves 8-10

2 matjas herring fillets (not marinated herrings)
1 onion
1 apple
3 sprigs parsley
salt
freshly ground black pepper
1 cup sour cream
½ cup plain Greek-type yoghurt
GARNISH
6 black olives
1 tablespoon chopped parsley

● 1. Cut the herring fillets into 3-4 pieces, place them in the work bowl and process for 5 seconds.
2. Cut the onion and the peeled apple into chunks and add to the herring, process for 3 seconds.
3. Add the remaining ingredients except the garnish and process for 3-5 seconds.
4. Transfer to a bowl and refrigerate for 2 hours. Serve on a decorative dish, garnished with olives and chopped parsley.

Hoummus Tahini or Chick Pea Dip

Serves 6

1 cup dried chick peas
juice of 3-4 lemons
2 cloves garlic
salt
⅛ teaspoon cayenne pepper
½ cup tahini paste (obtainable in
   some delicatessen shops)
½ tablespoon paprika for garnish

1. Soak the chick peas in water overnight.
2. Cook them for 1½-2 hours or until soft. Drain and keep
   some peas for garnish.
● 3. Place the peas in the work bowl and process until puréed.
● 4. Add the remaining ingredients and process until smooth
   in texture.
5. Place it in a bowl, garnish with some chick peas and
   paprika and serve with Lebanese bread.

Mousses

Chicken Liver Mousse

500 g (1 lb) chicken livers
3 shallots, chopped
30 g (1 oz) butter
¼ cup brandy
1 tablespoon honey
¼ cup cream
2 sprigs fresh thyme and
   marjoram
½ teaspoon salt
⅛ teaspoon freshly ground black
   pepper
125 g (4 oz) melted butter

1. Clean the livers and sauté together with the shallots.
● 2. Place them in the work bowl.
3. Pour the brandy and the honey into the sauté pan and
   reduce to 3 tablespoons, pour into the work bowl.
● 4. Add the remaining ingredients and process until very fine
   in texture.
5. Place the mousse into a bowl or jar, cover with some
   plastic film and refrigerate overnight.

Salmon Mousse

Serves 6-8

6 shallots
15 g (½ oz) butter
3 cups white wine flavoured fish
   stock
15 g (½ oz) gelatine softened in
   dry white wine
750 g (1½ lb) tinned salmon
3 tablespoons brandy
salt
freshly ground black pepper
⅛ teaspoon nutmeg
¾ cup fresh cream, whisked

1. In a saucepan lightly sauté the roughly chopped shallots.
2. Add the fish stock and the gelatine mixture, simmer for 1
   minute.
● 3. Pour into the work bowl, add the salmon, the brandy, the
   salt, the pepper and the nutmeg, process until all
   ingredients are puréed. Cool.
4. Whisk the cream until stiff, add to the work bowl and
   process only long enough to incorporate into salmon
   mixture.
5. Pour into a decorative mould and refrigerate for several
   hours and then turn out.

Fish Mousse (Quenelle Mixture)

Quenelles, little delicate dumplings made from fish, poultry or veal are one of the greatest creations of the French cuisine. The basic preparation can be either individually shaped and poached or it can be placed into individual soufflé dishes when it will end up as a mousse. Served with a Mousseline Sabayon Sauce it can be served as a delectable elegant main course. All ingredients must be well chilled.

Serves 6-8

1 kg (2 lb) white fish fillets (schnapper or gemfish are particularly good)
4 egg whites
¼ teaspoon nutmeg
½ teaspoon salt
¼ teaspoon cayenne pepper
600 ml (1 pint) fresh cream

● 1. In work bowl, a little at a time, process the fish to a very fine purée.
● 2. Add the egg whites, the seasoning and process for 20 seconds.
3. Put the mixture in a bowl and refrigerate for 2-3 hours.
4. Preheat the oven to 180°C (350°F).
● 5. Return the mixture to the work bowl and incorporate the chilled cream, process for 20 seconds.
6. Butter individual soufflé dishes and fill them with the mixture to within 2 cm (½ in) of the top.
7. Place the dishes into a roasting pan approximately 5 cm (2 in) deep, filled with enough water to reach halfway up the soufflé dishes.
8. Cover the roasting pan with aluminium foil. On the stove top bring the water to the boil. Bake for 30 minutes by which time the mousse should have risen like a soufflé.
9. Unmould and serve with either a Mousseline Sabayon Sauce (page 20) or a Pipi Sauce (page 27).

Pâtés and Terrines

Pork and Veal Terrine Stuffing

This stuffing, or *farce* as it is called in French, is the basis for most terrines. Used with strips of veal and ham it becomes the classical Terrine de Pork, Veau, and Jambon. It can be combined with the livers of chicken, calf, lamb, pork or beef. Baked with a short pastry crust it is called Pâté en Croûte. Most French households have developed their own 'Pâté Maison' and the best of them are unforgettable.

Yields about 1 kg (2 lb)

2 onions
30 g (1 oz) butter
¾ cup brandy, port or Madeira
375 g (¾ lb) each lean pork, lean veal
250 g (½ lb) fresh pork fat
2 lightly beaten eggs
1½ teaspoons salt
⅛ teaspoon pepper
⅛ teaspoon mixed spices
2 sprigs fresh thyme
½ clove garlic

● 1. In the work bowl, finely chop the onions.
2. Sauté them lightly.
● 3. Roughly cut the meat and pork fat. Place in the work bowl, 1½ cups at a time, and mince finely.
● 4. In the work bowl or in a large mixing bowl combine all ingredients. If necessary adjust seasoning.

Top and Bottom: Chicken Liver Terrine à la Bressane (page 50);
Right: Pork and Veal Terrine (page 48).

Chicken Liver Terrine à la Bressane

A very simple dish to prepare but the result is one of the most delicate baked chicken terrines.

Serves 4-6

½ clove garlic
3 sprigs parsley
300 g (10 oz) chicken livers
75 g (2½ oz) plain flour
4 whole eggs
4 egg yolks
3 tablespoons fresh cream
750 ml (1½ pints) milk
salt
freshly ground black pepper
⅛ teaspoon nutmeg

1. Preheat the oven to 160°C (325°F).
● 2. Place the garlic and the parsley in the work bowl and chop finely.
● 3. Add the rest of the ingredients in 2-3 lots and process finely.
4. Pour the mixture into an oval or rectangular terrine. Place the terrine in a pan of water on top of the stove and bring the water to boil.
5. Place in the oven and bake for 45 minutes. Test to see if cooked by inserting a skewer, it should come out dry. The terrine should also start coming away from the sides of the mould.
6. Serve hot, cut in slices and masked with Aurora Sauce (page 24).

Game Pâté

Now that game birds such as pheasant, guinea fowl, wild duck and venison from New Zealand are available, a game pâté is not any longer just a dream.

Yields about 1½ kg (3 lb)

½ kg (1 lb) boneless, raw game meat

MARINADE
½ cup brandy
1 cup red wine
2 tablespoons white wine vinegar
½ teaspoon salt
¼ teaspoon freshly ground black pepper
1 sprig each thyme, rosemary and marjoram
¼ teaspoon mixed spice
1 onion

STUFFING
3-4 slices of rindless bacon
1 kg (2 lb) Pork and Veal Terrine Stuffing (page 48)
1 bay leaf

● 1. Combine all ingredients of the marinade and process in the work bowl for 5 seconds.
2. Cut the game meat into 2 cm (½ in) cubes and marinate them for 12 hours.
3. Preheat the oven to 180°C (350°F).
4. Boil the marinade, reduce it to 1 cup and add it to the stuffing.
5. Line the bottom and sides of the terrine with the bacon. Spread some of the stuffing on the bottom of the terrine, then cover it with some of the marinated game meat. Alternate with 3 layers of each and at the top finish off with a layer of stuffing. Cover with some bacon and decorate with a bay leaf. Cover with a lid or some aluminium foil.
6. Place the terrine in 2½ cm (1 in) of hot water in a baking dish.
7. Place in the oven and cook for about 1½ hours. Insert a skewer to check if cooked. The juice which flows out should be clear.
8. To cool, take the terrine out of the pan. Remove the lid or aluminium cover and place a weight of 1½-2 kg (3-4 lb) on top of the terrine. Chill in refrigerator before serving.

Fish and Seafood

Fish and seafood are very much part of our daily meals. The processor will permit the preparation of many favourite dishes, some we previously never dared to attempt, therefore providing the variety and change sometimes needed.

Baked Stuffed Trout

A very elegant dish using the fish mousse-quenelle mixture for the stuffing and served with a calvados flavoured sauce.

Serves 4

4 250 g (¼ lb) fresh trout
250 g (¼ lb) fish mousse
   mixture (page 48)
30 g (1 oz) butter
⅛ cup dry white wine
juice of half a lemon
4 tablespoons fresh cream
2 egg yolks
4 tablespoons calvados brandy
salt
⅛ teaspoon cayenne

1. Preheat the oven to 180°C (350°F).
2. **Prepare the fish mousse stuffing and divide it into 4 parts.**
3. Place the stuffing in the cavity of each trout.
4. Butter a baking dish and place the trout next to each other and pour in the white wine and lemon juice.
5. Place in the oven and cook for about 20 minutes.
6. Strain the cooking liquid into a saucepan, add the cream, the egg yolks and the calvados and stir with a whisk. Season and serve poured over the trout.

Stuffed Fillet of Silver Dory, Gratinée

Serves 6

400 g (13 oz) mushrooms
4 shallots
4 sprigs parsley
1 medium onion
90 g (3 oz) butter
salt
freshly ground black pepper
6 large silver dory fillets
½ cup plain flour
2 eggs and ½ cup milk lightly
   mixed together
1 cup breadcrumbs
90 g (3 oz) butter
3 tablespoons cooking oil
2 tablespoons plain flour
1 cup dry white wine
1 cup fresh cream
1 cup grated Swiss-type cheese

● 1. In the work bowl finely chop the mushrooms, the shallots, the parsley and the onion.
   2. Sauté in the butter for 5 minutes.
● 3. Return to work bowl and chop until very fine.
   4. Season and spread over the fillets.
   5. Roll up the fillets and secure them with some toothpicks.
   6. Roll them in the flour, dip in egg-milk mixture and coat in breadcrumbs.
   7. Fry the fillets on medium flame in the butter-oil mixture for about 10 minutes until golden brown. Keep hot.
   8. Add 2 tablespoons of plain flour to the pan and cook for 2-3 minutes.
   9. Add the wine and cook for 5 minutes.
10. Add the cream and season.
11. Preheat the grill.
12. Arrange the fish on a gratin dish, pour the sauce over it and sprinkle with the cheese.
13. Place under a grill and brown.

Fish Croquettes Gratinés, à la Parisienne

Serves 6

CROQUETTES
500 g (1 lb) cooked fish fillets
1 cup fresh breadcrumbs
4 eggs
3 tablespoons fresh cream
3 sprigs parsley
juice of ½ lemon
salt
freshly ground black pepper
2 tablespoons water
½ cup of flour

SAUCE
45 g (1½ oz) butter
45 g (1½ oz) flour
½ cup dry white wine
¾ cup milk
2 egg yolks
¾ cup cream
juice of ½ lemon
salt
freshly ground black pepper
2 tablespoons grated Swiss-type
  cheese
30 g (1 oz) butter cut into pieces

● 1. Place all ingredients except ½ cup of breadcrumbs, 2 eggs and the cooking oil in the work bowl and process until fine in texture. Taste and adjust seasoning.
2. Combine 2 eggs with 2-3 tablespoons of water, and on two separate plates place the flour and the breadcrumbs.
3. Form the fish mixture into croquettes 5 cm (2 in) long and 2½ cm (1 in) in diameter.
4. First roll it in the flour, then dip it in the egg-water mixture and finally coat it in breadcrumbs.
5. Heat the oil to about 190°C (375°F) and cook the croquettes until golden brown.

SAUCE
1. Melt the butter and with the flour make a roux, cook for 5 minutes.
2. Heat wine and milk and add to the roux.
● 3. In the work bowl combine the egg yolks, the cream and the lemon juice, process for 5 seconds.
4. Gradually add the yolk cream mixture to the sauce, stir until smooth, season.
5. Arrange the croquettes on a gratin dish, coat with the sauce, sprinkle with the cheese and dot with pieces of butter.
6. Place under preheated grill until golden brown.

Fillets of Fish with Juliennes of Vegetables

Serves 6

60 g (2 oz) butter
2 shallots, finely chopped
6 fillets of fish
salt
freshly ground black pepper
1½ cups white wine flavoured
  fish stock (page 18)
1 carrot
2 leeks, white part only (or 2
  onions)
2 stalks celery

1. Preheat oven to 180°C (350°F).
2. Butter a baking dish, arrange the fish fillets, season, dot with pieces of butter and ¾ cover with fish stock.
3. On top of the stove bring the stock to simmering point, then put the dish in the oven for 10 minutes.
● 4. While the fish is poaching cut the carrots and the celery in the work bowl with the julienne disc or shredder. With a sharp knife halve the onion and cut into thin slices.
5. Slowly cook the juliennes of vegetable in butter until they are tender but not soft.
6. When the fish is cooked pour the stock over the vegetables and if necessary season.
7. Serve the poached fish fillets on preheated plates with the juliennes arranged on top of the fillets and the liquid poured over the fish.

Kulebaika (page 54).

Kulebiaka, Flaky Salmon Loaf

A regal dish for elegant occasions. The processor makes easy work of an otherwise gigantic task.

Serves 8-10

PASTRY
500 g (1 lb) plain flour
250 g (½ lb) chilled butter
90 g (3 oz) chilled vegetable fat
1 teaspoon salt
8 to 10 tablespoons iced water

SALMON FILLING
125 g (4 oz) butter
250 g (½ lb) fresh mushrooms
  sliced thinly
juice of 1 lemon
freshly ground black pepper
375 g (12 oz) onions, chopped
100 g (3½ oz) long-grain rice
¾ cup chicken stock (page 18)
6 sprigs fresh dill leaves
3 hardboiled eggs
1¼ kg (2½ lb) tinned red salmon
1 egg and 2 tablespoons water for
  glazing
1-1½ cups sour cream for serving

PASTRY
- 1. For the pastry combine the flour, chilled butter, the vegetable fat cut into cubes and the salt in the work bowl. Process for some 10 seconds until it has the texture of breadcrumbs.
- 2. Add the chilled water all at once and process only for a few seconds until the pastry starts to form a ball.
3. Remove the pastry on to a sheet of aluminium foil, press into a ball and refrigerate for 1-2 hours or until firm.

SALMON FILLING
1. Melt 30 g (1 oz) butter in a frying pan, add the mushrooms and cook for 3-4 minutes until the mushrooms are soft. Transfer to a bowl and sprinkle with the lemon juice.
- 2. In the work bowl finely chop the onions.
3. Melt 60 g (2 oz) butter in the frying pan and add all but 1 tablespoon of the chopped onions, cook for 3-5 minutes until the onions are soft and golden in colour. Season and add them to the mushrooms.
4. Melt the rest of the butter and cook the remaining onions for 2-3 minutes, add the rice and cook for 2-3 minutes stirring constantly.
5. Pour in the chicken stock, bring to the boil, cover and simmer for 12 minutes or until the water is absorbed and the rice is cooked.
6. Add the rice and the chopped dill to the mushrooms.
- 7. In work bowl chop the hardboiled eggs, add to the rice mixture.
8. With a fork break up the salmon and combine with rest of the ingredients, lightly mix together. Season.

TO ASSEMBLE
1. Preheat the oven to 200°C (400°F).
2. Divide the pastry approximately into two equal parts.
3. On a floured surface roll out a rectangle of pastry about 3-4 mm (¼ in) thick and 18 cm (7 in) wide by 40 cm (16 in) long.
4. Butter a rectangular baking tray, drape the pastry over a rolling-pin and unroll it on to the baking tray.
5. Place the filling along the length of the pastry leaving an edge of exposed pastry 2½ cm (1 in) wide all around.
6. Brush the exposed edge with the egg-water mixture.
7. Roll out the remaining pastry into a rectangle 23 cm (9 in) wide and 45 cm (18 in) long. Drape over the rolling pin and unroll over the filling.
8. Seal the edge, pressing the two sheets of pastry with the blade of a knife and turn the border of pastry to form a ridge around the filling. With the reverse side of the knife make shallow cuts in the edge.
9. In the centre of the pastry cut a circular opening 2½ cm (1 in) in diameter. From the scraps of pastry make some

decorative leaves, brush the pastry with the egg-water mixture and decorate the top. Refrigerate the Kulebiaka for 30 minutes.

10. Bake in the middle of oven for 1 hour or until golden brown. Serve cut into slices with some sour cream.

Jewfish with Pickle Sauce

Serves 4

1 2-2½ kg (4-5 lb) jewfish
6 slices of lemon
1 sprig each thyme, tarragon and marjoram
2 sprigs parsley
salt
freshly ground black pepper
SAUCE
1 onion
2 tomatoes, peeled
1 capsicum
2 tablespoons capers
½ cup of mixed pickled vegetables
1 dill cucumber, pickled
1 cup dry white wine
salt
freshly ground black pepper
1 cup sour cream

1. Preheat the oven to 180°C (350°F).
2. Butter a baking dish large enough for the fish.
3. Place them on the dish, with a sharp knife make 3-4 incisions in the upperside of the fish.
4. Arrange the lemon slices next to each other on top of the fish.
5. In the work bowl chop the herbs and sprinkle them on the fish. Season.
6. In the work bowl finely chop the onion, the tomatoes, the capsicum, the capers and pickles.
7. Mix them with the wine and pour the mixture into the baking dish around the fish.
8. Place in the oven and bake for 40 minutes.
9. When cooked transfer the fish on to a serving dish.
10. Add the sour cream to the pan juices. Taste and adjust the seasoning and if necessary add more cream.
11. Pour the sauce around the fish and serve.

Poultry

Many superb poultry dishes, together with their stuffings and sauces, are quickly and easily accomplished with the help of the processor.

Stuffed Chicken Drumsticks

This very tasty dish was adapted from Widrel Guerard's *Cuisine Minceur*.

Serves 6

12 chicken drumsticks
250 g (½ lb) mushrooms
1 onion
30 g (1 oz) butter
4 sprigs marjoram
¼ cup port
½ cup breadcrumbs
1 egg
freshly ground black pepper
salt
2 lambs brains
1 litre (2 pints) water
1 tablespoon white vinegar
1 cup dry white wine
3-4 cups chicken stock
1 cup of Madeira
2 tablespoons butter
2 tablespoons flour
2 carrots
2 onions
3 stalks celery
1 litre (2 pints) water
salt

1. Preheat the oven to 160°C (325°F).
2. Bone the chicken drumsticks by cutting the meat away from the bone at the thick end of the drumstick. Scraping the knife against the bone cut the meat away until the lower joint is reached. Pull and peel away the meat with the whole of the bone protruding. With a cleaver cut the drumstick bone close to the joint.
3. In the work bowl finely chop the mushrooms, the onion and the marjoram.
4. Sauté them in some butter and add the port. Cook for 5 minutes.
5. Draw away from the heat and add the breadcrumbs and the egg.
6. Blanch the brains for 5 minutes in the water and vinegar.
7. Chop them in the work bowl and add to the onion-mushroom mixture. Make sure the consistency is fairly dry and if necessary add more breadcrumbs. Season.
8. Fill the cavity of the drumsticks with the stuffing and place them on a buttered baking dish.
9. Pour in the white wine and the chicken stock and season.
10. Cover the dish with aluminium foil, place in the oven and cook for 45 minutes.
11. Strain the cooking liquid into a saucepan and keep the drumstick warm.
12. To the liquid add 1 cup of Madeira and reduce to 3 cups.
13. In the work bowl combine the butter and the flour and stir in to the reduced cooking liquid. If necessary adjust the consistency of the sauce with some chicken stock. Season.
14. In the work bowl with the julienne disc or shredder cut the carrots and the celery stalks. Cut the onions in half and chop with a knife. Blanch the juliennes in some salt water for 4 minutes.
15. Serve the drumsticks on a bed of juliennes of vegetables masked with the sauce.

Stuffed Chicken Drumsticks with Juliennes of Vegetables.

Chicken Quenelles (Boudin de Volaille)

In the preparation of the Chicken Quenelles the quantities and the technique are the same as for Fish Mousse (Quenelle mixture) (page 48), except the fish is replaced with chicken fillets.

Serves 6-8

1. Bring salty water to simmering point in a 5 cm (2 in) deep roasting pan.
2. To form the quenelles use two tablespoons. Dip them in hot water, pick up some of the mixture with one spoon and form the top with the other.
3. Push the formed quenelles, which should be almond shaped, from the spoon into salty water.
4. Gently poach them for 5 minutes turning them once.
5. Arrange the quenelles on preheated individual plates and serve them with any one of the bechamél or velouté based sauces such as Sauce Aurora (page 24) or Soubise (page 24).

Oyster-Stuffed Roast Chicken

Serves 4

2 small (no. 6-8) chickens
30 g (1 oz) butter
2 onions
2 stalks celery
1 large green or red capsicum
4 sprigs parsley
90 g (3 oz) butter
2 cups breadcrumbs from stale bread
freshly ground black pepper
salt
2 dozen oysters
½ cup cranberry preserve

1. Preheat oven to 215°C (425°F).
2. Rub the chickens with softened butter, salt and pepper and place them breast up, into a roasting dish.
● 3. In the work bowl finely chop the vegetables and the parsley.
4. Place them in the roasting dish around the chickens.
5. Roast the chickens for 45 minutes making sure that the temperature is reduced to 180°C (350°F) after the first 10 minutes. Baste occasionally with some melted butter.
6. When the chickens are done split them in half down the middle.
● 7. In the work bowl make coarse breadcrumbs from some stale bread.
● 8. To breadcrumbs in the work bowl, add the vegetables and the cooking juices, season and process for a few seconds.
● 9. Add some oyster liquid, but not so much as to make the stuffing sloppy.
10. Transfer the stuffing to a bowl and mix in the oysters.
11. In the roasting dish place the halves of chicken with the cavities up and fill them with the stuffing. Dot them with pieces of butter.
12. Reduce the oven to 130°C (250°F) and cook for approximately 15 minutes. If not golden brown place them under a preheated grill until coloured.
13. Accompany each serving with 2 tablespoons of cranberry preserve.

Stuffed Supremes of Chicken, Boitelle

This very delicate dish shows how the chicken quenelle mixture can be used as a stuffing.

Serves 4

4 supremes of chicken (chicken breasts)
- 6 tablespoons of chicken quenelle mixture (page 9) for stuffing
- 2 tablespoons of mushroom purée for stuffing
freshly ground black pepper
salt
60 g (2 oz) butter
juice of one lemon
1 cup fresh cream
1 tablespoon flour
4 sprigs parsley
2½ cup mushroom purée

1. Preheat oven to 200°C (400°F).
2. With a sharp knife cut a pocket as large as possible into each supreme.
3. Combine the quenelle mixture with 2 tablespoons of the mushroom purée and place a quarter of the stuffing into the cavity of each supreme.
4. Rub each supreme with some lemon juice, salt and pepper and roll them in butter which has been melted in a casserole.
5. Cover the supremes with aluminium foil, cover the casserole and place them in the oven.
6. After 6 minutes, check if the supremes are cooked, if not return for a few more minutes.
7. Remove the supremes and keep warm while making the sauce.
8. In the work bowl combine the cream and the flour and pour into the cooking liquid. Simmer gently for 3 minutes, stirring constantly. Season.
9. To serve, strain the sauce over the supremes and sprinkle with parsley which previously has been chopped in the work bowl. Serve the remainder of the mushroom purée as a garnish in the centre of the plate.

Braised Duckling with Apricot and Sausage Stuffing

Serves 4

2 small ducklings (no. 10 or 11)
cooking oil
500 g (1 lb) pork sausage mince
500 g (1 lb) dried dessert apricots
1 tablespoon sugar
¼ teaspoon cinnamon
¼ teaspoon salt
2 sprigs thyme
2 tablespoons brandy
½ cup port
½ cup beef stock (page 18)
freshly ground black pepper
salt
500 ml (1 pint) dry white wine
500 ml (1 pint) beef stock

1. Preheat the oven to 180°C (350°F).
2. Cut each duckling in half lengthwise.
3. Heat some cooking oil in a heavy bottomed frying pan or casserole and brown the ducklings. Set aside.
4. In same pan sauté sausage mince until lightly brown.
5. Place in the work bowl and add half the apricots, sugar, cinnamon, salt, thyme and brandy. Process for 10 seconds until all ingredients are combined.
6. Boil port and half cup beef stock until reduced to ½ cup, add to the stuffing and season.
7. Place the halves of duckling in a roasting dish with the cavities up and fill them with the stuffing.
8. Pour the white wine and remaining beef stock around the ducklings and season the braising liquid.
9. Cover the dish with aluminium foil.
10. Place in the oven and braise for 1½ hours.
11. Remove the ducklings and keep hot.
12. Reduce the braising liquid to 2 cups. Season and serve unthickened with the ducklings. Arrange the remaining apricots around the ducklings.

Meat

The meat dishes in this chapter show how the processor can be used to enhance and complement their flavour. Various stuffings, sauces and garnishes are prepared in a fraction of the time previously needed and give the imaginative cook more time to create a memorable meal.

Mushroom Veal Paupiettes

Serves 4

8 thinly beaten veal escalopes, about 15 x 10 cm (6 x 4 in)
200 g (7 oz) mushrooms
1 onion
30 g (1 oz) butter
400 g (13 oz) minced veal and pork mixture
2 egg whites
1 cup fresh cream
freshly ground black pepper
salt
60 g (2 oz) butter
2 cups veal or beef stock
1½ cups Duxelles Sauce (page 26)

1. Preheat oven to 180°C (350°F).
● 2. In the work bowl chop the mushrooms and the onions finely.
3. Sauté them in the butter until most of the mixture has evaporated.
● 4. Place the minced meat into the work bowl and process until very fine.
● 5. Add the egg whites and process for 10 seconds.
● 6. Gradually add the cream and process for a further 10 seconds.
● 7. Add the mushrooms, season and work for a few seconds to combine.
8. Divide the stuffing into 8 equal parts, spread it over the veal. Roll the meat and secure with toothpicks and tie with some twine.
9. In butter brown the paupiettes of veal.
10. Arrange them on a roasting pan and pour in the stock, season.
11. Cover the pan with aluminium foil.
12. Place in the oven and braise for 45-60 minutes or until the meat is tender. Serve with Duxelles Sauce.
Note: Use the braising liquid in the making of the Duxelles Sauce (page 26)

Steak Tartare

The processor makes an exceptionally good Steak Tartare as it permits the meat to be freshly minced to a very fine texture.

Serves 4

1 kg (2 lb) trimmed beef, fillet or rump are best
4 egg yolks
6 teaspoons salt
6 teaspoons freshly ground black pepper
3 tablespoons capers
●4 tablespoons finely chopped onions
●4 tablespoons finely chopped parsley
●4 tablespoons finely chopped chives

● 1. Cut the meat into rough cubes and 1½ cups at a time, mince finely in the work bowl.
2. On individual plates shape the meat into 4 mounds.
3. Make a well in each and place an unbroken egg yolk in each one.
4. Arrange all the other ingredients on individual serving dishes or saucers, They will then be mixed at the table to the diner's individual taste.

Top to bottom: Fricadelles (page 63); Stuffed Fillet of Pork in Filo pastry (page 62); Steak Tartare (page 60).

Fillet of Beef à L'Amiral

Serves 4

1 kg (2 lb) beef fillet, in one piece
2 rashers of bacon
2 onions
4 sprigs parsley
30 g (1 oz) butter
6 fillets of anchovy
1 egg
freshly ground black pepper
1 cup dry red wine

1. Preheat oven to 200°C (400°F).
● 2. In work bowl chop the bacon, the onions and the parsley.
3. Lightly sauté, put in a bowl, add the egg, season and mix well together. Salt should not be necessary as the anchovies are sufficiently salty.
4. At 3 cm (1½ in) intervals along the length of the fillet, make incisions without cutting through the fillet.
5. Place some of the stuffing into each pocket and then bind the fillet so that the stuffing stays in place.
6. Next roast the fillet for 30-45 minutes, depending on the degree of cooking desired.
7. Remove the fillet from the roasting dish and deep warm.
8. On top of the stove heat the cooking juices in the roasting pan, add the red wine and cook for a few minutes. Season.
9. Cut the fillet into slices, making the incisions between each pocket of stuffing. Pour the cooking juice over each and serve with some steamed vegetables.

Stuffed Fillet of Pork in Filo Pastry

Serves 4

1 onion
2 stalks celery
1 carrot
½ clove garlic
2 sprigs thyme or marjoram
45 g (1½ oz) butter
freshly ground black pepper
salt
1 cup dessert prunes, pitted
½ cup dry white wine
2 tablespoons honey
½ cup breadcrumbs
4 pieces of pork fillet, about 200 g (7 oz) each
8 sheets filo pastry
¼ cup melted butter

1. Preheat oven to 190°C (375°F).
● 2. In work bowl finely chop the vegetables, the garlic and the herbs.
3. In a saucepan, using some of the butter sauté the vegetables.
● 4. In the work bowl finely chop the prunes and add to the vegetables, continue to sauté, add the wine, the honey and the breadcrumbs, cook for a further 5 minutes. Season.
5. In a frying pan using the rest of the butter lightly brown the fillets.
6. Spread out the filo pastry, two sheets for each fillet, place the fillet on the pastry and cover the fillet with the stuffing.
7. Fold the sides of the pastry over the fillet and roll the fillet in the pastry.
8. Brush the pastry with the melted butter and arrange the wrapped fillets on a baking tray.
9. Bake until the pastry is golden brown, about 20-25 minutes.

Stuffed Leg of Lamb in Puff Pastry—Gigot d'Agneau en Crôute

Serves 6

1 leg of lamb 1½ kg (3 lb) after boning
2 lamb kidneys
250 g (4 oz) mushrooms
60 g (2 oz) chicken liver pâté (if not available continental liverwurst may be used)
2 tablespoons brandy
½ cup fine dry breadcrumbs
1 teaspoon salt
freshly ground black pepper
1-2 packets frozen puff pastry
1 egg and 3 tablespoons water for glazing

1. Ask the butcher to bone and butterfly the leg of lamb making sure that the meat is as little cut about as possible, it should form a large, flat slab of meat.
2. Preheat the oven to 160°C (325°F).
● 3. In the work bowl place the kidneys which have been cut into rough cubes. Process for 5-8 seconds.
● 4. Add the remaining ingredients and process until combined but not too fine.
5. Spread the stuffing over the meat and neatly roll the meat. Using butcher's twine tie the roll at 5 cm (2 in) intervals.
6. Roast for 45 minutes.
7. Take out of the oven and permit to cool.
8. Heat the oven to 190°C (375°F).
9. Cut the roll into slices 2 cm (¾ in) thick. Each slice should contain some of the stuffing.
10. On a floured surface roll out defrosted pastry into a strip about 25 cm (10 in) wide. Cut it in 20-25 cm (8-10 in) long pieces. On each place a slice of the meat. Brush the edges and fold them over to form an envelope.
11. Reverse the wrapped meat until the smooth side is up. In the centre cut a small hole and glaze the pastry with the lightly beaten egg-water mixture. Decorate with some pastry leaves.
12. Bake the pieces for about 20 minutes or until the pastry is light brown.

Meat Fricadelles

Meat Fricadelles are croquettes made from cooked meats in which meat leftovers can be used.

Serves 4

600 g (1¼ lb) cooked meat or meat leftovers
300 g (10 oz) mashed potatoes
1 onion
4 sprigs parsley
2 eggs
freshly ground black pepper
salt
½ cup plain flour
2 eggs and 2 tablespoons water mixed together
1 cup fine breadcrumbs
60 g (2 oz) butter
¼ cup cooking oil

● 1. Chop the onion and parsley finely in the work bowl, set aside.
● 2. In the work bowl, 2 cups at a time, finely mince the cooked meat.
● 3. Add the onion and the parsley, the potatoes and mix in the eggs and season.
4. Form the mixture into cylindrical croquettes about 3½-4 cm (1½ in) in diameter and about 7½ cm (3 in) long.
5. Dust them in flour, dip in the egg-water mixture and roll in the breadcrumbs.
6. Fry in butter until golden brown.

Vegetables

The more effort that goes into a vegetable dish, the better it looks and tastes. That time-consuming chopping, slicing, shredding and grating, the mixing and making of juliennes can now be achieved quickly. In seconds you can make gourmet dishes that once would have taken hours.

Stuffed Artichokes au Gratin

Serves 6

3-4 litres (6-8 pints) water
salt
6 large artichokes
juice of one lemon

STUFFING
1 onion
2 shallots
2 sprigs oregano
3 sprigs parsley
½ clove garlic
30 g (1 oz) butter
½ cup dry vermouth
½ cup breadcrumbs
freshly ground black pepper
salt
90 g (3 oz) grated Swiss-type
  cheese

1. Preheat oven to 180°C (350°F).
2. In a large saucepan boil the salted water.
3. With a sharp knife trim about 2½ cm (1 in) off the tops of the leaves.
4. Rub the cut areas and the bottom of the artichokes with lemon juice to prevent discoloration.
5. Drop them into the boiling water and cook for 10 minutes.
6. In the meantime finely chop the onion, the shallots, the oregano, parsley and garlic in the work bowl.
7. Lightly sauté in the butter add the vermouth and cook for 5 minutes, add the breadcrumbs and season.
8. When the artichokes are cooked and cool enough to handle, part the leaves slightly, divide the stuffing into 6 parts and insert between the leaves.
9. Arrange the artichokes on a roasting dish, pour in some water and cover with aluminium foil.
10. Place in the oven, cook for 30 minutes.
11. Remove them from the oven, sprinkle with the cheese, previously grated in the work bowl and brown them under a preheated grill. Serve as an entrée.

Purée of Cauliflower and Watercress with Cream

Serves 4-6

1 medium-sized head of
  cauliflower
1 bunch of watercress
2 cups thick Béchamel Sauce
½ cup cream
60 g (2 oz) grated Swiss-type
  cheese
freshly ground pepper
salt
2 tablespoons fine dry
  breadcrumbs mixed with 2
  tablespoons grated Swiss-
  type cheese
30 g (1 oz) melted butter

1. Preheat the oven to 190°C (375°F).
2. Break up the cauliflower into flowerets and discard the stem. Cut the rough stems from the watercress (save for watercress soup).
3. Bring the water to the boil. Drop the cauliflower in and boil slowly for 6 minutes. Add the watercress leaves and boil for a further 5 minutes. Drain.
4. In the work bowl, 2 cups at a time, finely purée the vegetables.
5. In a mixing bowl gradually combine the purée, the Béchamel, the Swiss cheese and season to taste.
6. Pour the purée into a baking dish, sprinkle with cheese and breadcrumb mix and the butter.
7. Bake for about 30 minutes until brown.

Clockwise from top: Polish Beetroot Puree; German Potato Dumplings (page 68); Spinach Purée (page 67).

Brussels Sprouts Mould

A light first course or luncheon dish. It can also be served as a vegetable with roast veal or chicken.

Serves 6

1 onion
15 g (½ oz) butter
60 g (2 oz) grated Swiss-type cheese
60 g (2 oz) white breadcrumbs
5 eggs
1¼ cups milk, heated with 60 g (2 oz) butter
¼ teaspoon salt
⅛ teaspoon nutmeg
1½ kg (3 lb) Brussels sprouts
3-4 litres (6-8 pints) water
salt

1. Preheat oven to 160°C (325°F).
2. In the work bowl finely chop the onion.
3. Lightly sauté in the butter and scrape into the work bowl.
4. Add the cheese, the breadcrumbs and the eggs, process until all ingredients are mixed.
5. Gradually add the hot milk and butter, transfer to a mixing bowl.
6. In a saucepan blanch the Brussels sprouts in boiling salted water for 7-10 minutes.
7. In the work bowl, 2 cups at a time, finely chop the Brussels sprouts.
8. Fold the chopped Brussels sprouts into the cheese mixture.
9. Butter a mould or soufflé dish and fill it with the mixture.
10. Place the mixture in a roasting-dish filled with some boiling water.
11. Bake for about 40 minutes. Make sure the dish is cooked by inserting a knife into the centre, it should come out clean.
12. Remove the mould from the roasting dish and let stand for 10 minutes, run the knife around the edges and turn out onto a serving dish.

Casserole of Carrots with Onions and Garlic— Carrottes à la Concierge

Can be served as a vegetable or a light meatless main course.

Serves 6

750 g (1½ lb) carrots
250 g (½ lb) onions
3 tablespoons cooking oil
1 clove garlic, crushed
15 g (½ oz) plain flour
½ cup beef stock (page 18)
½ cup boiling milk
salt
freshly ground black pepper
1 teaspoon sugar
¼ teaspoon nutmeg
2 egg yolks
¼ cup fresh cream
2 tablespoons parsley, chopped

1. In the work bowl, using the slicing disc, slice the carrots and the onions.
2. Slowly cook the vegetables in the oil for 30 minutes without browning them, add the crushed garlic in the last 5 minutes of cooking.
3. Add the flour and cook for another 3 minutes.
4. Add the stock and the milk, season and cook uncovered for 20 minutes until liquid has reduced to about a third.
5. Away from heat mix in the egg yolks and the cream.
6. Return to low heat to thicken the liquid. Do not boil.
7. Serve in a vegetable dish sprinkled with parsley.

Spinach Purée with Onions, Capsicum and Ham

Serves 4-6

2 litres (4 pints) water
750 g (1½ lb) spinach
2 onions
60 g (2 oz) butter
⅛ teaspoon nutmeg
freshly ground pepper
salt
juice of one lemon
½ cup sour cream
2 capsicum, coarsely chopped
½ cup of ham cut into small dice

1. Boil the water and blanch the spinach for 5 minutes. Drain and cool it under running cold water. Squeeze out excess water.
● 2. In a large frying pan sauté the onions, previously chopped in the work bowl, add the spinach and dry it out.
3. In the work bowl finely purée the spinach, add the lemon juice and the sour cream. Season.
4. Put the purée into a saucepan, add the chopped capsicum and diced ham and heat.

Braised Celery with Bacon and Apples

Serves 4

1 bunch celery
30 g (1 oz) butter
2 rashers smoked bacon
½ cup chicken or beef stock (page 18)
½ teaspoon crushed juniper berries
juice of one lemon
1 apple, diced
½ teaspoon salt
freshly ground black pepper

● 1. In the work bowl, using the slicing disc, slice the celery.
● 2. Sauté the bacon which has been previously chopped in the work bowl, add the celery, and sauté for about 5 minutes.
3. Add the stock, the juniper berries, the lemon juice, the apple and the seasoning and cook for 5 minutes.

Turnip and Potato Purée

Serves 6

1 kg (2 lb) turnips
30 g (1 oz) butter
1 cup chicken or beef stock
salt
freshly ground black pepper
500 g (1 lb) mashed potatoes
60 g (2 oz) butter
2 tablespoons chopped parsley

● 1. In the work bowl slice the turnips.
2. Lightly sauté them in the butter, add the stock and braise for 20 minutes.
● 3. In the work bowl purée the turnips and combine with the mashed potatoes, add the butter, season and serve in a vegetable dish sprinkled with chopped parsley.

Polish Beetroot Purée

An unusual vegetable to be served with lamb, venison or hare.

Serves 4

4 medium beetroot
2 litres (4 pints) water mixed with
   ½ cup vinegar
100 g (3½ oz) smoked pork fat
   (speck)
2 tablespoons sugar
½ teaspoon salt
freshly ground black pepper
juice of ½ lemon
3 tablespoons sour cream

1. Place the beetroot in the saucepan of cold water and vinegar.
2. Slowly bring to the boil and simmer for 30 minutes or until soft when pierced with a fork.
3. Permit the beetroot to cool in the water.
4. When cool enough to handle peel the beetroot. Cut them into pieces which fit into the feed tube of the work bowl.
5. Grate the beetroot in the work bowl.
6. Cut the pork fat into small dice and fry until crisp and brown.
7. In mixing bowl combine all the ingredients. Season and serve hot to accompany meat.

German Potato Dumplings

Makes 15 to 20 dumplings

150 g (5 oz) butter
125 g (4 oz) dried white
   breadcrumbs
3 slices white bread
750 g (1½ lb) peeled potatoes
60 g (2 oz) plain flour
90 g (3 oz) semolina
3 teaspoons salt
⅛ teaspoon nutmeg
⅛ teaspoon white pepper
2 eggs

1. Melt and heat 125 g (4 oz) of the butter in a frying pan.
2. Add the breadcrumbs and stirring constantly fry until they are light brown. Set aside.
3. Cut the crust off the bread slices and cut into 1¼ cm (½ in) squares and fry them golden brown in the butter. If necessary add some more butter. Drain them on some kitchen paper and set aside.
● 4. Cook the potatoes until soft, place them in the work bowl and process until mashed.
● 5. Add the flour, the semolina, 1 teaspoon of salt, the nutmeg and the pepper. Process until all ingredients are combined.
6. In a mixing bowl lightly beat the eggs with a fork and add to the work bowl.
● 7. Process until incorporated. If the mixture is too thin add some more flour a teaspoon at a time.
8. Take the mixture out of the work bowl, flour your hands and shape the dumplings into balls about 5 cm (2 in) in diameter. With a finger make a hole and insert 3-4 of the sippets (bread squares). Press the hole closed.
9. Half fill a saucepan with water, add 2 teaspoons of salt and bring to the boil. Drop in the dumplings making sure they do not stick to each other. Gently simmer for about 15 minutes until the dumplings rise to the surface.
10. Remove with perforated spoon, arrange on a serving dish and serve sprinkled with the fried bread crumbs.

Left to right: Zucchini and Roasted Almond Salad (page 70); Rainbow Salad; Mango Vinaigrette (page 71).

Salads

Because of their versatility and attractive appearance, salads are ever popular as side dishes, accompaniments and main meals. Preparation, however, can be long and tedious as there is much chopping, slicing and grating involved. Once again the processor comes into its own, reducing the work to a fraction, but always providing a perfect result.

Celery, Apple and Raisins, Sauce Remoulade

Serves 4

1 bunch of celery
2 apples
¼ cup raisins

SAUCE REMOULADE
¾ cup mayonnaise (page 21)
1 teaspoon anchovy paste
3 tablespoons mixed pickles
1 tablespoon capers
1 sprig each thyme, tarragon, parsley

● 1. In work bowl, with the slicing disc, slice the celery stalks and the apple cut in squares.
   2. Place in a salad bowl and add the raisins.
● 3. In the work bowl, using the steel blade, add all the sauce ingredients and process for a few seconds until the pickles are chopped, but not too fine.
   4. Pour the Remoulade Sauce over the salad, toss and serve.

Zucchini with Roasted Almonds

Serves 4

750 g (1½ lb) zucchini
small bunch of chives
2 sprigs fresh dill
½ cup Vinaigrette à la Creme (page 22)
½ cup whole almonds, roasted

● 1. In the work bowl, through the feed tube, using the slicing disc, slice the zucchini.
● 2. In the work bowl, using the steel blade, finely chop the chives and the dill.
   3. In a salad bowl combine the zucchini, the chives and dill.
   4. Add the vinaigrette and toss. Refrigerate for 1 hour before serving to marinate the zucchini. Just before serving mix in the almonds.

Avocado Purée Salad

Serves 4

2 ripe avocados cut into halves
juice of 1 lemon
2 tablespoons walnuts
salt
freshly ground black pepper
1 stalk celery
2 tablespoons raisins
4 black olives

   1. Cut the avocados in half and with a spoon carefully scoop the flesh into the work bowl. Save the skins.
● 2. In the work bowl, using the steel blade, purée the avocados.
● 3. Add the lemon juice, the walnuts, the celery and season, process for 5 seconds.
   4. Transfer to a mixing bowl, and add the raisins. Mix well.
   5. Place the avocado purée back into the shells and smooth out on top. Serve garnished with a black olive.

Mango Vinaigrette

4 mangos, peeled and cut into
   large slivers
1 capsicum
2 shallots
1 stalk celery
6-8 mint leaves
¼ cup vinaigrette, made with
   lemon juice (page 22)

Serves 4

● 1. In the work bowl, through the feed tube and using the
      slicing disc, slice the mangos. Set to one side.
● 2. In the work bowl, using the steel blade, combine
      vinaigrette and remaining ingredients, but save 4 mint
      leaves for garnish.
   3. In a shallow serving bowl combine the sliced mango and
      the vinaigrette, garnish with the remaining mint leaves.

Rainbow Salad

2 carrots
1 turnip
1 beetroot
2 apples
4 stalks celery
½ cup vinaigrette made with
   lemon instead of vinegar (page
   22)

Serves 4-6

● 1. In the work bowl, using the julienne disc or shredder, cut
      all the vegetables except the celery.
● 2. In the work bowl, using the steel blade, chop the celery.
   3. Combine all vegetables in a salad bowl and pour in the
      vinaigrette. Toss well and serve.

Fresh Cucumber Cream Salad

3 medium cucumbers, peeled
salt
½ cup sour cream
juice of 1 lemon
1 teaspoon sugar
freshly ground black pepper
1 tablespoon chopped chives for
   garnish

Serves 4

● 1. In the work bowl through the feed tube and using the
      slicing disc, slice the cucumbers.
   2. Place them in a bowl and sprinkle with salt. Stand for ½
      hour then put the sliced cucumbers in a sieve or colander
      and drain the liquid.
● 3. In the work bowl, place the cream, lemon juice, the sugar,
      and the pepper, process to combine.
   4. Arrange the cucumber on a shallow serving plate, mask
      with the cream and garnish with chopped chives.

Desserts

'Last minute' preparation of some desserts is made possible and the quality will be superior to anything previously attempted. Variations on familiar themes are endless and an attempt at something new will end in success. At all times the freshness of all dishes is retained.

Mangos in Champagne

Serves 4-6

2-3 medium mangos, peeled and cut into large slivers
1 punnet fresh strawberries, about 200 g (7 oz)
3 tablespoons kirsch
½ bottle chilled dry champagne

● 1. In the work bowl, using the slicing disc, cut the mangos into slivers. If the mango is too ripe cut with a knife.
● 2. In the work bowl, using the steel blade, purée the strawberries and add the kirsch.
3. Use 4 chilled champagne glasses or glass dessert bowls. In the bottom place the strawberry purée, on top of it arrange the small slivers of mango and fill the glasses with champagne.

Rockmelon with Strawberry Cream

Serves 4

300 ml (½ pint) fresh cream, chilled
2 punnets of strawberries, about 500 g (1 lb)
100 g (3½ oz) caster sugar
3 tablespoons kirsch
2 small ripe rockmelons, chilled

● 1. Pour the cream into the work bowl and process until it starts to thicken. Watch carefully, do not beat it too much.
● 2. Add the cleaned strawberries (saving 4 for garnish), the sugar and the kirsch and process for about 10 seconds until the strawberries are puréed.
3. Peel the melons, cut them in halves and remove seeds. Cut them into thin half-moon shaped slices and arrange them in a decorative fashion on 4 dessert plates.
4. Divide the strawberry cream into 4 parts and heap it in the centre of each plate. Garnish with a strawberry and serve with chilled dry champagne.

Any Fruit or Berry Sorbet

Serves 6

500 g (1 lb) fruit or berries
250 g (½ lb) sugar
juice of 1 or 2 lemons
1-1¼ cups water
2 egg whites

● 1. In the work bowl process the fruit or berries until puréed.
● 2. Add the sugar and the lemon juice. Add the water only if the purée is not sufficiently liquid, as may be the case with apples or melons.
3. Strain the purée through a sieve, place in a container and freeze until almost solid.
● 4. Return to the work bowl and process until smooth.
● 5. Beat the egg whites until stiff. Add them to the purée and process for a few seconds until incorporated.
6. Return the sorbet to the freezer and freeze overnight.

Top to bottom: Three sorbets, mango, strawberry, Chinese gooseberry (page 72); fruit sauces (page 75); Mango in Champagne (page 72). Dessert Pancakes (page 74).

Gratin of Sautéed Pears

Serves 6

1¼ kg (2½ lb) crisp pears
75 g (2½ oz) butter
125 g (4 oz) plum jam
2 tablespoons rum
60 g (2 oz) butter
90 g (3 oz) sugar
3 egg yolks
1 tablespoon flour
½ teaspoon cinnamon
60 g (2 oz) fresh brown
   breadcrumbs
2 egg whites
½ tablespoon sugar
icing sugar

1. Preheat the oven to 160°C (325°F).
2. Peel, core and quarter the pears.
● 3. In the work bowl using the slicing disc, slice the pears.
4. Sauté them one layer at a time in 75 g (2½ oz) of hot butter, until light brown on both sides. Place them in a baking dish.
5. Melt the jam, add the rum and carefully fold into the pears.
● 6. In the work bowl, using the steel blade, cream the butter and 90 g (3 oz) of sugar. Gradually beat in the egg yolks, the flour, the cinnamon and finally the breadcrumbs.
7. Beat the egg whites stiff, add the sugar. In a mixing bowl fold the egg white into the breadcrumb mixture and spread it over the pears.
8. Place in oven and bake for 25 minutes or until the top has puffed up, sprinkle with some icing sugar and continue baking for another 25 minutes.
9. Allow to cool and refrigerate.

Note: This dish is best eaten the next day.

Dessert Pancakes

Makes 10-12, 15 cm (6 in) in diameter

PANCAKE BATTER
½ cup milk
½ cup water
3 egg yolks
1 tablespoon sugar
3 tablespoons brandy, rum or
   orange liqueur
150 g (5 oz) flour
2 tablespoons melted butter
½ tablespoon butter, ½
   tablespoon cooking oil for
   frying

ORANGE-ALMOND BUTTER
100 g (3 oz) sugar
1 tablespoon grated orange zest
250 g (½ lb) butter
½ cup fresh orange juice
3 tablespoons orange liqueur
¼ cup brandy for flaming
100 g (3 oz) almonds or
   macaroons
¼ teaspoon almond extract

● 1. Set the processor going and put the pancake ingredients into the work bowl in the order listed. Process for a few seconds until well combined. Refrigerate for 1-2 hrs before using.
2. Fry pancakes in a crepe pan as described on page 43.
● 3. In the work bowl combine sugar, the grated zest and the butter and process until creamed.
4. Gradually add the orange juice and the liqueur. Add the almonds or the macaroons and process until they are chopped and incorporated.
5. Spread the orange-almond butter on the pancakes, heat in pan and serve folded or rolled, flaming with brandy.

Variation: Substitute fresh fruit, e.g. strawberries for orange almond butter.

Apple Caramel Mould

Serves 6

2 kg (4 lb) crisp cooking apples
¼ teaspoon cinnamon
grated peel of 1 lemon
90 g (3 oz) sugar
¼ cup calvados apple brandy or
brandy
60 g (2 oz) butter
4 eggs
1 egg white
CARAMEL
90 g (3 oz) sugar
2 tablespoons water
GARNISH
¼ cup brandy
1½ cups whipped cream,
flavoured with sugar and a few
drops of vanilla essence

1. Preheat the oven to 200°C (400°F).
2. Peel, core and cut the apples into large dice and cook on a low heat for 20 minutes until tender, stir occasionally.
3. Add the cinnamon, the grated lemon peel and the sugar, continue cooking until the purée is thick enough to hold its shape.
● 4. Remove from heat, place in the work bowl, process, add the brandy and then one at a time the eggs and finally the egg white.
5. Line a mould with caramel by boiling the sugar and the water in the mould over moderate heat until the syrup caramelises. At once dip into cold water to cool slightly. Tilt the mould to cover all internal surfaces. Again dip in cold water to set the caramel.
6. Fill the caramel lined mould with the apple mixture. Cover, place in a pan of boiling water. The water should reach up the side of the bowl to the level of the apple mixture.
7. Place in the oven and simmer for 1-1½ hours until it shrinks away from the sides.
8. To serve cold, refrigerate for 4-5 hours, run the knife around the edge of the mould, reverse the mould on to a serving plate and let stand until it comes away from the dish.
9. Heat the brandy and rinse out the remaining caramel from the mould. Pour it over the dessert. Serve with whipped cream.

Fruit Sauces

Fruit Sauces are used with ice creams, custard desserts and puddings. They are made from fresh or frozen fruits or berries.

Strawberry or Raspberry Sauce

Yield 1½ cups

500 g (1 lb) strawberries or
raspberries
250 g (½ lb) castor sugar
2 tablespoons brandy or kirsch
juice of one lemon

● 1. Combine all ingredients and process in work bowl until puréed and the sugar is dissolved.
2. Strain through a sieve and pour over the dessert.

Cakes and Pastry

Linzer Cake

185 g (6 oz) plain flour
⅛ teaspoon ground cloves
¼ teaspoon cinnamon
185 g (6 oz) unblanched almonds
125 g (4 oz) sugar
1 teaspoon grated lemon peel
250 g (½ lb) butter, softened
2 egg yolks, lightly beaten
1 teaspoon vanilla essence
2 hard-boiled egg yolks
1¼ cups thick raspberry jam
1 egg, well beaten
2 tablespoons fresh cream
icing sugar

Makes one 23 cm (9 in) cake

● 1. In the work bowl place the flour, the cloves, the cinnamon, the almonds which have been previously finely ground in the work bowl, the sugar and the lemon peel, process and add the butter, the lightly beaten egg yolks and the vanilla essence. Process for 5 seconds, add the hard-boiled egg yolks and process until mixture is smooth and doughy.
2. Wrap the dough in plastic film and refrigerate for 1 hour, until firm.
3. Preheat the oven to 180°C (350°F).
4. Take out ¾ of the dough and return the rest to the refrigerator.
5. Lightly butter a spring-form cake tin. Place the dough in and with your fingers press it out to cover the bottom and the sides.
6. Spread the jam evenly over the bottom of the shell.
7. Roll out the rest of the dough and cut it into strips 1 cm (½ in) wide. Cut it into lengths to form diagonal strips, spaced about 2½ cm (1 in) and placed over the jam.
8. Loosen the top edge of the shell away from the tin and fold it over the edge of the jam to form a rim.
9. Lightly beat the egg with the cream and brush all the pastry parts.
10. Bake for 45-50 minutes or until light brown.
11. Slip the rim of the tin off the cake and cool for 10 minutes. Sprinkle with icing sugar and serve.

Shortbread with Roasted Almonds

185 g (6 oz) plain flour
60 g (2 oz) sugar
125 g (4 oz) butter, chilled
5 drops vanilla essence
2 tablespoons castor sugar for sprinkling
2 tablespoons chopped, roasted almonds

Makes one 15-18 cm (6-7 in) shortbread

1. Preheat oven to 150°C (300°F).
● 2. Place all ingredients in the work bowl and process until dough forms a ball, approximately 5-10 seconds, turning the processor on and off several times. Do not over-process.
3. Turn the pastry on to a floured surface and roll out to the diameter of the flan.
4. Place it in the flan and press down into a flat cake.
5. Prick the shortcake with a fork and bake for one hour in the oven.
6. Sprinkle with castor sugar and leave to cool.

Top to bottom: Linzer Cake (page 76); Clafouti with Mango (page 78); Shortbread with Roasted Almonds and Peanut Butter Cookies (pages 76, 79); Linzer Cake slice.

Clafouti with Mango

A very simple cake and almost any fruit may be used.

Serves 6-8

1¼ cups milk
60 g (2 oz) sugar
3 eggs
1 tablespoon vanilla essence
75 g (2½ oz) plain flour
375 g (¾ lb) mango flesh (3-4 mangos) cut in small chunks
60 g (2 oz) sugar
icing sugar
12 whole hazelnuts for decoration

1. Preheat oven to 180°C (350°F).
● 2. Place all ingredients except the mango and the last quantity of sugar and icing sugar into the work bowl and process until combined.
3. Use a 4 cm (1½ in) deep baking tin or pie dish and pour a layer approximately 5 mm (¼ in) of the batter on the bottom.
4. Place it over moderate heat for 1 minute until it sets.
5. Remove from heat and spread mango over the batter.
6. Sprinkle with the remaining sugar and pour the remainder of the batter over.
7. Bake for 1 hour.
8. Serve hot or warm sprinkled with icing sugar.

Peanut Butter Cookies

Makes 60

⅓ cup butter or margarine
¼ cup creamy or crunchy peanut butter
¾ cup sugar
1 egg
2 cups self-raising flour
½ teaspoon cinnamon
½ cup roasted blanched peanuts

● 1. In the work bowl, cream the butter, the peanut butter and the sugar, add the egg and process for 10 seconds.
● 2. Add the flour and the cinnamon. Process until mixed.
● 3. Add the peanuts which have been previously finely chopped in the work bowl.
4. On a sheet of aluminium foil form a roll about 5 cm (2 in) in diameter, wrap and refrigerate for several hours until firm.
5. Preheat oven to 190°C (375°F).
6. Cut the roll 3 mm (⅛ in) thick and place 2½ cm (1 in) apart on an ungreased baking tray.
7. Bake for 6-8 minutes until light brown. Cool on the tray for 1 minute, transfer to wire rack and cool.

Short-Crust Pastry (Pâte Brisée)

For savoury tarts and quiches

Makes one 20-23 cm (8-9 in) flan

200 g (7 oz) plain flour
¼ teaspoon salt
125 g (4 oz) butter, chilled
3-4 tablespoons cold water

● 1. Place the flour, the salt and the butter cut into cubes in the work bowl and process until the consistency of breadcrumbs.
● 2. Add the water all at once and process until the pastry forms a ball. Do not over-process.
3. Place the pastry on to a floured surface and roll out in a circle slightly larger than the flan.
4. Roll the pastry on to the rolling pin and then unroll into the flan. Press against the bottom and sides. Bake according to recipe selected.

Sweet Short-Crust Pastry (Pâte Sablée)

For fruit tarts, sweet pies and desserts.

Makes one 20-23 cm (8-9 in) flan

200 g (7 oz) plain flour
¼ cup sugar
130 g (4 oz) butter
1 egg mixed with 1-3 tablespoons
cold water

The method of preparation is the same as the short-crust pastry (Pâte Brisée).

Rough Puff Pastry

A very handy and quick way of making pastry pies and tarts. However it is not a proper puff pastry and has to be used as soon as it is made.

Enough for one small pie or tart

250 g (8 oz) self-raising flour
125 g (4 oz) chilled butter
½ teaspoon salt
2 tablespoons very cold water

● 1. Place the flour, the salt and the butter cut into cubes into the work bowl and process a few seconds until the texture of breadcrumbs.
● 2. Add the water and process until it forms a ball.
3. Place the pastry onto a floured surface and roll out forming a rectangle.
4. First fold the side on to the middle and then the top and bottom.
5. Press the edges to seal the air inside, refrigerate for 10 minutes.
6. Repeat the rolling and folding process and again refrigerate before using.

Index